Writing, Speaking, and Listening

Communicating in Real-Life Situations

by Elaine Dion, Ruth Fennick, and Mary Peters

illustrated by Don Ellens

cover by Linda Pierce

Publisher
Instructional Fair • TS Denison
Grand Rapids, Michigan 49544

Instructional Fair • TS Denison grants the individual purchaser permission to reproduce patterns and student activity materials in this book for noncommercial individual or classroom use only. Reproduction for an entire school or school system is strictly prohibited. No other part of this publication may be reproduced in whole or in part. No part of this publication may be reproduced for storage in a retrieval system, or transmitted in any form or by any means, electronic, mechanical, recording, or otherwise, without the prior written permission of the publisher. For information regarding permission, write to Instructional Fair • TS Denison, P.O. Box 1650, Grand Rapids, MI 49501.

ISBN: 1-56822-847-3
Writing, Speaking, and Listening
Copyright © 1999 by Ideal • Instructional Fair Publishing Group
a division of Tribune Education
2400 Turner Avenue NW
Grand Rapids, Michigan 49544

All Rights Reserved • Printed in the USA

Table of Contents

Chapter 1: Writing 1
    Social Notes 3
    E-mail Messages 9
    Friendly Letters 11
    Business Letters 13
    Envelopes 15
    Job Application Cover Letters 17
    Résumés 19
    Interview Follow-Up Letters 21
    Agendas 23
    Meeting Notes 25
    Brochures 27
    Web Home Pages 29

Chapter 2: Speaking 31
    Telephone Communication 33
    Requests for Information 37
    Complaints 39
    Solicitations 41
    Job Seeking 43
    Introductions 45
    Announcements 47
    Interviews 49
    Discussions 51
    Meetings 53
    Speeches 55
    Campaigns 59
    Honors 61

Chapter 3: Listening 63
    Directions and Messages 69
    One-on-One Conversation 73
    Group Discussion 77
    Speech and Lecture Notes 81
    Stories and Poems 85
    Broadcast Media 91

Introduction

Most students do not aspire to become famous orators or writers. However, they do need to be able to communicate in numerous ways, both with individuals and with groups, throughout their lives. In many different settings, they need to be able to listen effectively, and they need to competently express their thoughts and feelings in speech and writing. Many of these communication skills will eventually help them to advance in their careers or to participate more meaningfully in social and political arenas. The more immediate benefit, however, is the ability to learn effectively, think critically, and enrich personal relationships.

Page 33 of the IRA/NCTE Standards for the English Language Arts (1996) highlights the importance of this study:

> Throughout their lives, students will write and speak in widely differing social arenas: as informed citizens, as employees and co-workers, as neighbors. They will also use language as members of a family, for personal affirmation and reflection, and for cultural enrichment. In each instance, they will draw on their knowledge of language conventions as they adjust their speech and writing to respond to the needs of specific audiences, purposes, and situations.

This book focuses on communication strategies and conventions for situations that students confront in their daily lives. Three chapters address fundamentals of audience, purpose, and occasion in various writing, speaking, and listening situations. Activities help students to apply strategies to make their communication—personal or public—more active and more purposeful. Whether they are following directions, interviewing for a job, designing a Web page, using the telephone, or writing a sympathy note to a friend, students learn to analyze the communication situation and respond appropriately.

Name _____

Chapter 1: Writing

Forget about school writing for a moment. Think, instead, about the other writing you do. Maybe you wrote a note to a friend in study hall this morning about your weekend or a thank-you note to your aunt and uncle for the birthday money they sent you last week, or maybe last night you posted an e-mail on your favorite Internet board about the latest Leonardo DiCaprio film.

Assess Your Writing Needs

Look at the following list of common types of personal and public writing. In the second column, check those types that you have already written at some time in the past. Then think about your future writing and, in the third column, circle the word that indicates how often you think you will write each of these types of correspondence.

Types of Writing	Have Already Written	Will Need to Write in the Future
Thank-you notes		often occasionally never
Congratulatory notes		often occasionally never
Sympathy notes		often occasionally never
Invitations		often occasionally never
E-mail messages		often occasionally never
Friendly letters		often occasionally never
Business letters		often occasionally never
Résumés		often occasionally never
Meeting agendas		often occasionally never
Meeting notes		often occasionally never
Brochures		often occasionally never
World Wide Web pages		often occasionally never

The following pages focus on the above types of writing. Although you may not have prepared all of these documents in the past, you probably will in the future. The instructions, samples, and activities in this chapter will help you improve your skills in real-life correspondence.

© Instructional Fair • TS Denison   1   IF19304 Writing, Speaking, and Listening

Name _____

Purpose and Audience

In everything you write, *what* you say and *how* you say it are determined by two important elements common to all writing: purpose and audience. First of all, what you say is determined by your purpose—whether it is to bring your friend up-to-date on your social life or to thank your relatives. Secondly, your relationship with your audience—the person or people to whom you are writing—determines how you say something—what words you choose. Your choice of words determines your tone, which is usually defined as the writer's attitude. For example, if your attitude toward your aunt and uncle is formal, you may thank them for the "generous gift"; however, if it is informal, you may jokingly thank them for the "cash flow," giving your thank-you note a humorous tone.

Assess Your Tone

Your choice of formal or informal tone depends on your audience. Usually, correspondence with close friends and family is informal; correspondence with businesses and school personnel is formal. Think of writing that you have done recently. List three examples in the first column (include the audience). In the second, state your purpose for each piece of writing. In the last column, circle the tone you used in that writing. (Follow the model in number one.)

Type of Writing and Audience	Purpose	Tone
1. A note to my mom	To say I went to my friend's house	Formal or (Informal)
2.		Formal or Informal
3.		Formal or Informal
4.		Formal or Informal

Pen or Computer?

Audience and purpose also affect what writing medium you use—pen or computer, for example. When you write e-mail to an on-line pen pal, you use a computer. When you write a cover letter and résumé for a part-time job, you also use a computer. When you write a thank-you note for a job interview, you may write by hand to convey a personal tone that the computer cannot provide. List examples of writing that you would prepare by each medium.

On Computer	By Hand

Conventions

Finally, audience and purpose determine protocol—the conventions or accepted rules of style used by most people for various types of correspondence. From an ad for a bicycle to an Internet home page, standard practices guide writers. These conventions guide writers as they decide on form, content, punctuation, and word choices for specific occasions and audiences. However, these conventions are not hard and fast rules. In fact, as times change, writing conventions change. For example, electronic mail—now commonplace—has produced a whole new set of writing conventions, called *e-mail etiquette*. The next few pages will provide models, conventions, and writing activities to help you improve your everyday writing.

Name _____

Social Notes

Social notes express recognition of special occasions or achievements; thus, the term *noteworthy* is used to describe them. We send them to offer congratulations on birthdays and graduations, to invite people to parties, to express our appreciation for a gift or kindness, or just to say we appreciate a person's friendship.

The practice of sending notes is as old as paper itself, and some social notes have even become literary treasures. For example, the poems of the famous American poet Emily Dickinson were actually notes she sent to friends and loved ones. The Dickinson poem below was a thank-you note sent along with a flower. What do you think the poet was thanking her friend for? Explain your answer below or write your own thank-you poem. (If you like Emily Dickinson's poems, you will find more online at http://www.planet.net/pkrisxle/emily/poems Online.html.)

*I pay in satin cash—
You did not state your price.
A Petal, for a paragraph
Is near as I can guess.*

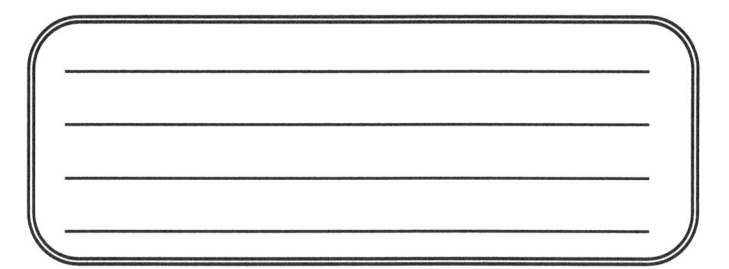

Emily Dickinson sent all of her notes by mail or messenger. Of course, she lived in the mid 1800s. Today we use two primary modes for sending social messages—electronic and postal. Notes sent through the mail may be handwritten or computer-generated. Handwritten notes communicate personalized messages, and, in spite of the convenience and efficiency of instant e-mail, the handwritten note is still very much appreciated (think how pleased you are to receive a handwritten note from a friend).

However, some people correspond entirely by computer, sending all of their notes electronically. Others write each note by hand. Some people create and save their own social notes on the computer and then send these personal designs rather than buying cards. Once again, audience and purpose govern these decisions. You probably would not choose to write e-mail to someone who dislikes using electronic mail; whereas, you could send e-mail to anyone who provided an online address on his or her stationery, advertising, or business cards.

YOU'RE INVITED!
Farewell
Thank You
Thinking of You
GET WELL

Name _____

Handwritten Notes

Most writers use the following conventions for writing notes by hand.
- Write neatly with a blue or black ink pen and use complete sentences.
- Leave margins of one inch on the top and bottom and on both sides.
- Write the date in the upper right corner (use standard abbreviations for months).
- Skip two lines, write the salutation (Dear _____,) at the left margin, and add a comma.
- Indent five spaces and begin by stating the reason for your note in the first sentence.
- Depending on the number of topics you want to cover in your note, it may be several sentences or several paragraphs. Change paragraphs whenever you change topics.
- Conclude your note gracefully in the last one or two sentences by summing up your reason for writing and wishing your reader well.
- Skip two lines, write a suitable closing with the first letter capitalized (Yours truly, Love, Your friend,) at the right margin, and end the line with a comma.
- Sign your name below the closing.
- If you wish to add a postscript (a line at the bottom), write P.S. at the left margin and write a short parting comment. Be certain to proofread your entire message.

Review the standard abbreviations for months by completing the chart below. Write out four-letter names; for those longer than four letters, use three-letter abbreviations, followed by a period.

1. Jan. _____
2. _____
3. _____
4. _____
5. _____
6. _____
7. July _____
8. _____
9. _____
10. _____
11. _____
12. _____

Envelopes

Whether you type or print an address and return address, use the following guidelines established by the U.S. Postal Service. Address the envelope below to a friend.

- ALL CAPITAL LETTERS (type or print)
- NO PUNCTUATION (none!)
- FOUR LINES FOR U.S. MAIL
- FIVE LINES FOR INTERNATIONAL
- TWO-LETTER STATE ABBREVIATIONS
- ABBREVIATIONS (ST, RD, AVE, BLVD)

© Instructional Fair • TS Denison
IF19304 Writing, Speaking, and Listening

Name _____

Thank-You Notes

Using standard conventions (page 4) and the model to the right, write a thank-you note of your own at the bottom of the page. Use one of the scenarios listed here or one of your own. Remember to make the language appropriate to your audience. You are the author—you determine the tone. It may be formal, informal, or even poetic!

- Your neighbors loaned you their lawnmower to finish your mowing jobs after your mower broke down.
- The new YMCA manager gave you an interview for your article in the paper.
- A recommendation from the principal got you the summer job you wanted.
- Your own: _____

> Jan 5, 1999
>
> Dear Aunt Ruth and Uncle Karel,
>   Thank you so much for the money for Christmas. I have already added your gift to the money I've put away for college (most of it anyway; I did keep some out for a new fashion magazine and a Tony Bennett CD.) My mom says to say hello and that she is looking forward to our next family get-together. I hope you are having a great year.
>
>   Love,
>   Annie

Try It!

Name _____

Congratulatory Notes

Following the conventions for social notes and the model to the right, compose a note of congratulations. Use one of the scenarios below or one of your own. Make your tone match your audience—formal or informal.

- Your cousin has graduated from medical school with honors.
- One of your favorite teachers has been named Teacher of the Year.
- Your great-grandfather just turned 95.
- A friend of yours placed first in a marathon.
- Your own: _____

> May 10, 1999
>
> Dear Michele,
>   Way to go, girl! I just heard that you made this year's all-conference soccer team. What an honor, and you deserve it. I can't wait to watch the all-stars in action. I'll be your number-one fan. Keep up the good work. I know you'll have a great season. C-ya!
>
>   Your best friend and fan,
>   Annie

Try It!

Name _____

Sympathy Notes

The most difficult note to write is the sympathy note. While conventions determine the format, as they do for all social notes, the writer must be more sensitive than usual to the audience who has suffered misfortune. The tone of a sympathy note must be sincere and serious.

Following the conventions you have learned for social notes and the model to the right, compose a sympathy note using one of the situations below or one of your own.

- A neighbor's grandfather has died after a long illness in the hospital.
- Your friend's family member was killed in an automobile accident.
- A child whose family lived on your street, but whom you never really knew, has died.
- Your own: _____
  _____

> October 1, 1999
>
> Dear Mr. and Mrs. Goodman and family,
>
> I was very sorry to hear about the death of your loved one. Mr. Snow was a very kind man, and I always looked forward to seeing him in his apple orchards each fall. He always let my sister and me try out all the apples before we decided which trees we would pick from. We also looked forward to the cider samples he always gave us.
>
> I will think of Mr. Snow every time I go by his orchards, and always remember him for his generosity and kindness to us.
>
> Sincerely,
> John Howard

Try It!

Name _____

Invitations

Parties and celebrations mean invitations, which are fun and easy to design, especially if you have access to a desktop publishing program. Invitations can be simple or fancy, traditional or funky, but whatever their style, they must still provide the basic information often referred to as the five "W's": what, where, when, who, and why. Use these conventions as well as an RSVP line (originally from the French expression, *Repondez, s'il vous plaît,* which means "a reply is requested"). An RSVP on an invitation asks for a reply within a certain time frame to let the host know who will be attending and who will not.

Think of a party that you would like to give. Create an outline below for your invitation. Include the basic information indicated on the outline, following the model below.

- What/Why
- Where
- When
- Given by whom
- RSVP
- (other information guests will need)

What:

Where:

When:

Host:

RSVP:

Bring:

A SPOOK-OUT

What: Halloween Camp Out

Where: Delps' Back Yard

When: Fri., Oct 30, 6:30 p.m. to Sat., Oct 31, 10:00 a.m.

Host: Erik Delp

RSVP: 815-496-0000 by Oct. 25

Bring: Sleeping bag and pillow and your tale of terror!

Try it! Now design your own invitation. Be creative with your own letter art and drawings. If you have access to a computer graphics program, design your page on computer.

Name _____

E-Mail Messages

E-mail Conventions or Netiquette

Much of today's social communication is electronic. The main difference between traditional and electronic mail is speed. Correct spelling, punctuation, and grammar are still very important, and the audience to whom you are writing still determines what language and tone—formal or informal—are appropriate. Politeness is also just as important in cyberspace as it is on paper. Use the e-mail conventions listed on the right and the model below to compose your own e-mail on the next page. Write a note for one of the scenarios listed on previous pages or create your own. (If you are already an e-mailer, create a message you intend to send.)

E-MAIL PROTOCOL
Avoid all caps, which means shouting.
Proofread/spell check before posting.
Keep sentences and paragraphs short.
Use white space to break up text.
Expressions include:
:-)	Smile
;-)	Wink
:-(	Frown
:-0	Laughter
BTW	By the way
WTG	Way to go
FAQ	Frequently asked question
ROTFL	Rolling on the floor Laughing

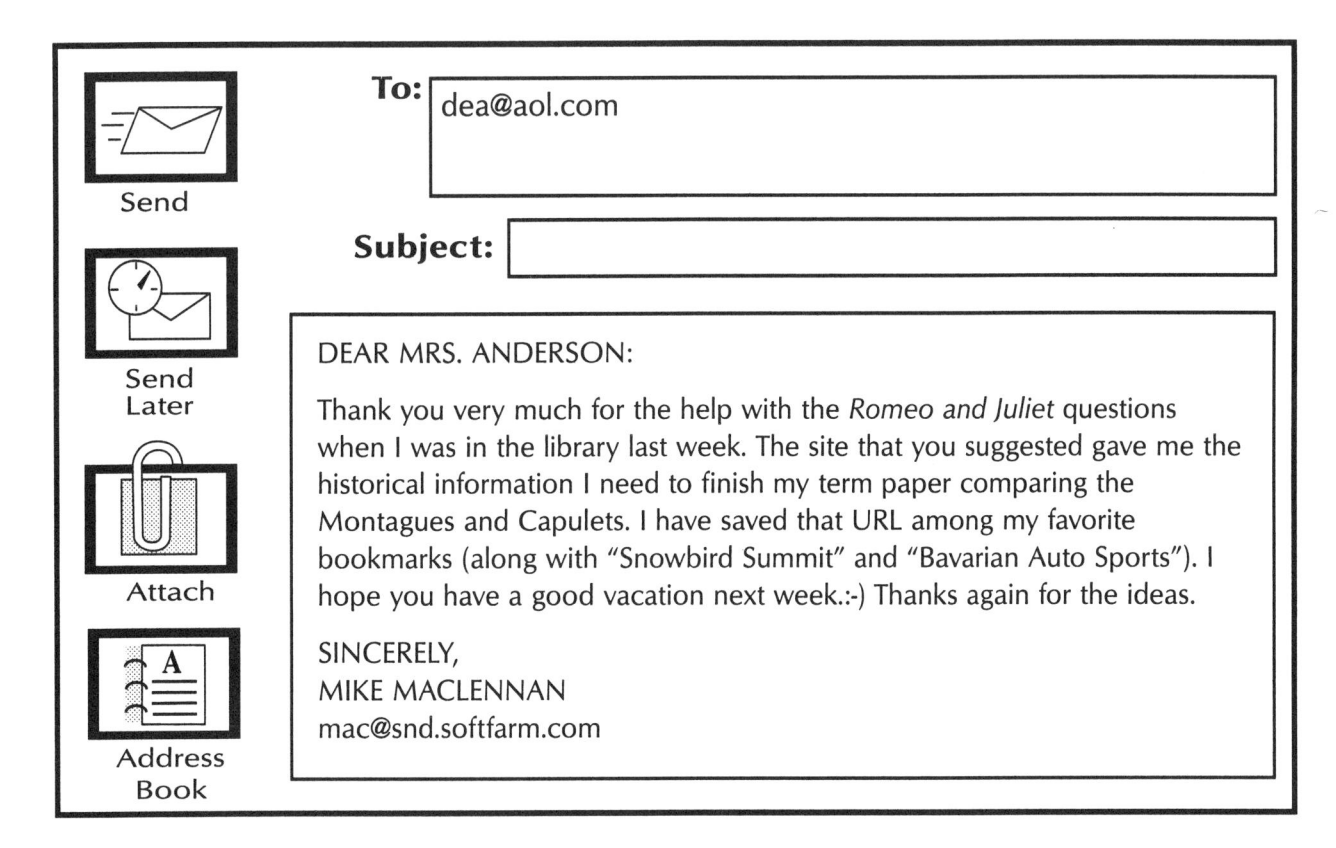

To: dea@aol.com

Subject: _____

DEAR MRS. ANDERSON:

Thank you very much for the help with the *Romeo and Juliet* questions when I was in the library last week. The site that you suggested gave me the historical information I need to finish my term paper comparing the Montagues and Capulets. I have saved that URL among my favorite bookmarks (along with "Snowbird Summit" and "Bavarian Auto Sports"). I hope you have a good vacation next week.:-) Thanks again for the ideas.

SINCERELY,
MIKE MACLENNAN
mac@snd.softfarm.com

Send
Send Later
Attach
Address Book

In the above subject box, write a logical heading. _____
If the receiver wanted to reply, what address would go in the box after To? _____
What error in e-mail protocol is apparent in this message? _____

Name _____

Try It!

Compose your own e-mail note below. (In the CC: box, add the name of someone you wish to send a carbon copy when you send this message.) Then use the checklist below to edit your message.

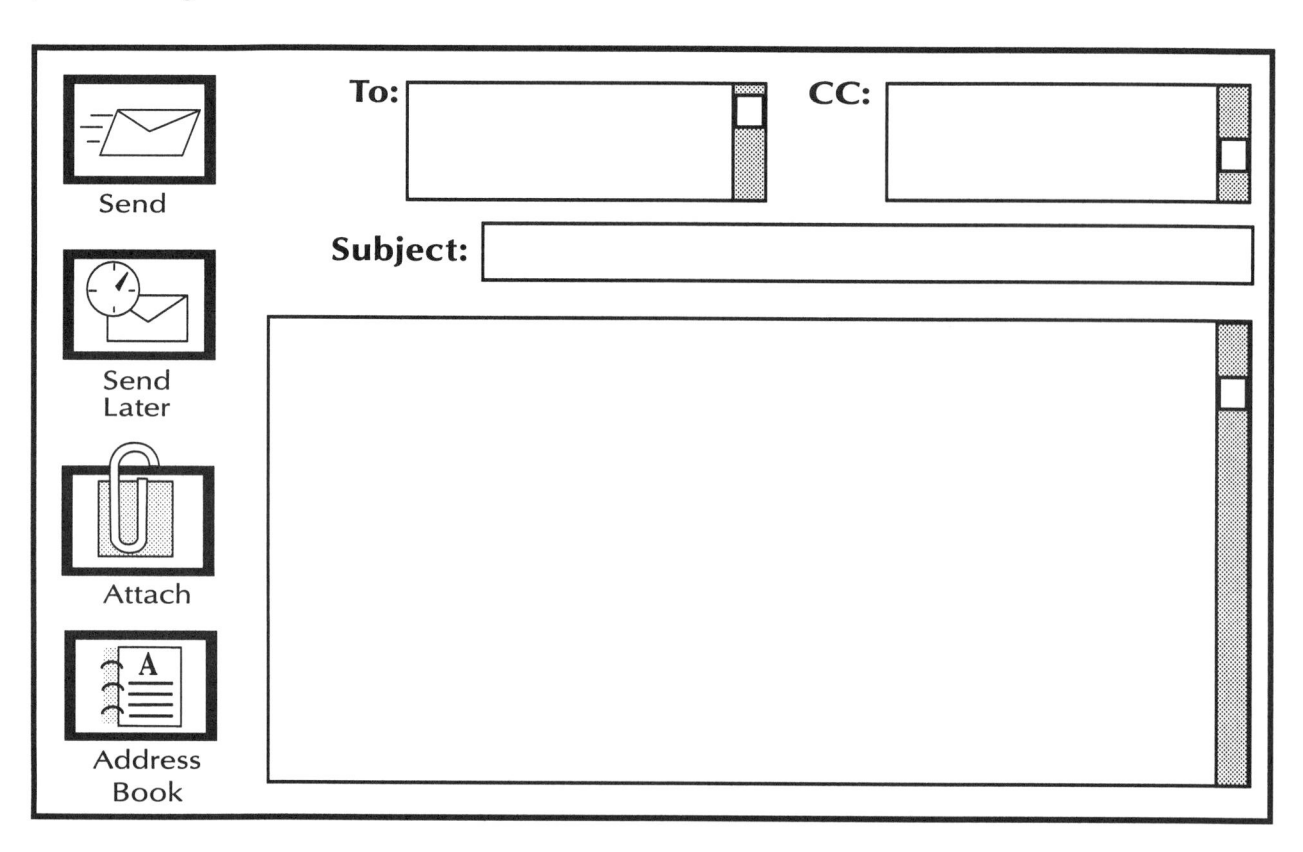

Checklist:
1. Have you used all lower case? _____
2. Are spelling, punctuation, and grammar correct? _____
3. Are sentences and paragraphs short? _____
4. Have you used white space to separate paragraphs? _____
5. Are the address and message clear and complete? _____
6. Is the language and tone appropriate to this audience (and the cc audience)? _____
7. Could anything in your message be misunderstood? _____

Remember, e-mail is instantaneous!
Pause a moment to double check before you push "send."

Name _____

Friendly Letters

Whether you write to your friends and family by e-mail or regular mail, using the standard conventions for a particular type of writing helps you and your reader. These conventions guide you as a writer and they also meet the expectations of your reader. Most writers observe the following conventions in writing personal letters.

- Supply full return address in the upper right-hand corner.
- Write the date below the address.
- Use a comma after the salutation.
- Indent each paragraph five spaces.
- Write the closing at the bottom right-hand side of the letter.
- Capitalize the first word of the closing.
- Sign underneath the closing.
- Add P.S. for postscript if desired.
- Write neatly and proofread and correct any errors before mailing.

Read the letter to the right. You will find four faults in conventions in this letter. Identify each of these faults below and explain the change needed.

---

239 Trelease
October 12, 1999

Dear Nick:
Thanks for your letter, girl. I don't receive a lot of letters (my mom and dad are terrible about writing) so I'm really excited every time a letter comes. I've read your jokes to everybody on my floor and posted them on our hall bulletin board. Can you believe it, you've been published in my dorm!

I hope you will be able to visit me here at U of I. It's a great school, in spite of its size. At first, the size frightened me—I mean 50,000 faces are hard to look at each day, especially when you come from rural nowhere and a school of 280 kids. Now that I'm used to the "sea of faces" everywhere I go, I'm realizing all the benefits. We have a class A basketball team; those games are really exciting. If you come this winter, I can get tickets in advance. We also have great concerts and plays. I saw *Cats* last week; it was just as good as the *Chicago* production, and it was free with my student card. What's more, my teachers are so good. I'm struggling to keep up because there's so much homework, but my art history class and my physiology class are so interesting that I actually love going to class.

The worst part of school is that I miss everybody, so please write again soon, and make plans to visit me—anytime! Just let me know when you're coming, and I'll meet you at the train station. Have to go now and study for tomorrow's chem. test.

love,
Shel

P.S. How is your media class going? Are you still interviewing and broadcasting for the whole junior high?

---

1. _____
2. _____
3. _____
4. _____

Name _____

Try It!

In the space below, compose a handwritten reply to the letter on the previous page or a letter of your own. Use the conventions listed on the previous page. Then, if you have access to a computer, prepare this letter on a word processor, observing one-inch margins, double-spacing between paragraphs, and single-spacing within paragraphs.

Name _____

Business Letters

Business letters require certain conventions expected by a business audience. There are more rules in business writing than in personal writing because professional people expect these conventions in their correspondence. Compare the two letters below—the first a personal letter, the other a business letter. Identify the conventions of the business letter that do not appear in the personal letter. List them below (check the list of business letter conventions printed on the following page).

---

239 Trelease
Urbana, IL 60180
October 11, 1999

Dear Nick,

Thanks for your letter, girl. I don't receive a lot of letters (my mom and dad are terrible about writing) so I'm really excited every time a letter comes. I've read your jokes to everybody on my floor and posted them on our hall bulletin board. Can you believe it, you've been published in my dorm!

I hope you will be able to visit me here at U of I. It's a great school, in spite of its size. At first, the size frightened me—I mean 50,000 faces are hard to look at each day, especially when you come from rural nowhere and a school of 280 kids. Now that I'm used to the "sea of faces" everywhere I go, I'm realizing all the benefits. We have a class A basketball team; those games are really exciting. If you come this winter, I can get tickets in advance. We also have great concerts and plays. I saw *Cats* last week; it was just as good as the Chicago production, and it was free with my student card. What's more, my teachers are so good. I'm struggling to keep up because there's so much homework, but my art history class and my physiology class are so interesting that I actually love going to class.

The worst part of school is that I miss everybody, so please write again soon, and make plans to visit me—anytime! Just let me know when you're coming, and I'll meet you at the train station. Have to go now and study for tomorrow's chem. test.

Love,
Shel

P.S. How is your media class going? Are you still interviewing and broadcasting for the whole junior high?

LYONS & COMPANY
1300 E. Fourth Street
Jonesville, IN 61301

July 23, 1999

Mr. John Egan
Director
Habitat for Humanity
PO Box 235
Scannel, IN 61301

Dear Mr. Egan:

I received your letter and the Habitat for Humanity "Welcome" packet in yesterday's mail, and I am very excited to be involved in this project. My co-workers and I look forward to helping your organization build a home for a needy family in our area. Our completed registration form is enclosed.

We will be available to participate in the August 13 activities, and we will also be available every Saturday after that through October. Please let us know what equipment we should bring with us next week and what time we should plan to arrive.

I will plan to see you at the board meeting on Tuesday evening, July 30. If there are any changes in the current schedule, please let me know.

Sincerely,

Mary Lyons
Mary Lyons
President
enc.
cc: Sharon Barton, President, Habitat for Humanity

---

1. _____
2. _____
3. _____

1. _____
2. _____
3. _____

Name _____

Try It!

Now write your own business letter in the frame on the right or use a word processor. Choose a scenario from one of the following. Then use the checklist below to be certain you have used the correct conventions.

- You are a school guidance counselor. Write a letter to a local employer recommending someone for a position with his or her company.
- You are a consumer. Write a letter to a company that has disappointed you with a faulty or poor product.

Your own scenario:

_____
_____
_____

1. _____ One-inch margins are maintained on both sides and top and bottom.
2. _____ Style is full-block with every line beginning at the left margin.
3. _____ Full return address is three or four lines at top left; date is on following line.
4. _____ Four to seven spaces follow date line (number of spaces varies depending on length of letter).
5. _____ Inside address contains name, title, company, street, city, state, and zip code.
6. _____ Double space before salutation (which should be placed about ⅓ page from top).
7. _____ Salutation (Dear Mr., Mrs., Ms., Sir, or Madame) is followed by a colon.
8. _____ Double space follows salutation.
9. _____ Double-spacing is used between paragraphs; single-spacing within paragraphs.
10. _____ First paragraph states purpose for writing.
11. _____ Middle paragraph or paragraphs explain and support that purpose.
12. _____ Last paragraph indicates the next step to be taken.
13. _____ First word of closing is capitalized (Yours truly, Sincerely,).
14. _____ A comma follows closing; signature is written underneath closing.
15. _____ Name is typed on the fourth line below closing (space is for signature).
16. _____ The abbreviation *enc.,* two spaces below typed name, indicates an enclosure.
17. _____ The abbreviation *cc:* followed by a name indicates to whom a copy has been sent.
18. _____ Spelling and grammar are correct.

Name _____

Envelopes

Addressing Envelopes

Whether you type or print, whether your mail is business or personal, use the following guidelines, which have been established by the U.S. Postal Service. For companies that send large volumes of mail (some send thousands of pieces of mail every week), these directives are regulations—their mail will not be delivered unless the addresses on their mailings conform to these rules. For other mailers, these conventions are only guidelines that the U.S. Postal Service asks us to use. Use the following guidelines to address the envelope below. (Use the address from the business letter you wrote, or make up a new one.)

- ALL CAPITAL LETTERS (type or print)
- NO PUNCTUATION (none!)
- FOUR LINES FOR U.S. MAIL
- FIVE LINES FOR INTERNATIONAL
- TWO-LETTER STATE ABBREVIATIONS
- ABBREVIATIONS (ST, RD, AVE, BLVD)

Postal Abbreviations

How many of the U.S. Postal abbreviations for states do you already know? Fill in the blanks.

Alabama		Hawaii		Massachusetts		New Mexico		South Dakota	
Alaska		Idaho		Michigan		New York		Tennessee	
Arizona		Illinois		Minnesota		North Carolina		Texas	
Arkansas		Indiana		Mississippi		North Dakota		Utah	
California		Iowa		Missouri		Ohio		Vermont	
Colorado		Kansas		Montana		Oklahoma		Virginia	
Connecticut		Kentucky		Nebraska		Oregon		Washington	
Delaware		Louisiana		Nevada		Pennsylvania		West Virginia	
Florida		Maine		New Hampshire		Rhode Island		Wisconsin	
Georgia		Maryland		New Jersey		South Carolina		Wyoming	

Folding a Business Letter

Folding and stuffing a business envelope seems a simple task. However, it is an important one. A correctly folded and stuffed letter positions the name of the person receiving the letter in his or her immediate view as the letter is opened. This convention, which is both practical and complimentary, confirms to the receiver that this letter is personally addressed to him or her.

Business letter stationery, which is eight and one-half inches wide and eleven inches long, fits conveniently inside a standard business envelope, which is nine and one-quarter inches wide. The length of a letter when folded into thirds is the approximate size of the envelope. To achieve the desired effect, the sender must follow the steps below.

1. Fold the bottom one third of the letter up (the bottom edge should be under the salutation).
2. Fold the top one third of the letter down, leaving the top fold about one-quarter inch shorter than the fold underneath it so that the edge is easy to grasp.
3. Stuff the letter so that when it comes out of the envelope, the top unfolds right side up. (The salutation and receiver's name, *Dear* _____, should be the first line the reader sees.)

Try It!

Now try these steps with a practice sheet of 8½" x 11" and a 4" x 9¼" envelope. Follow the three-step procedure below.

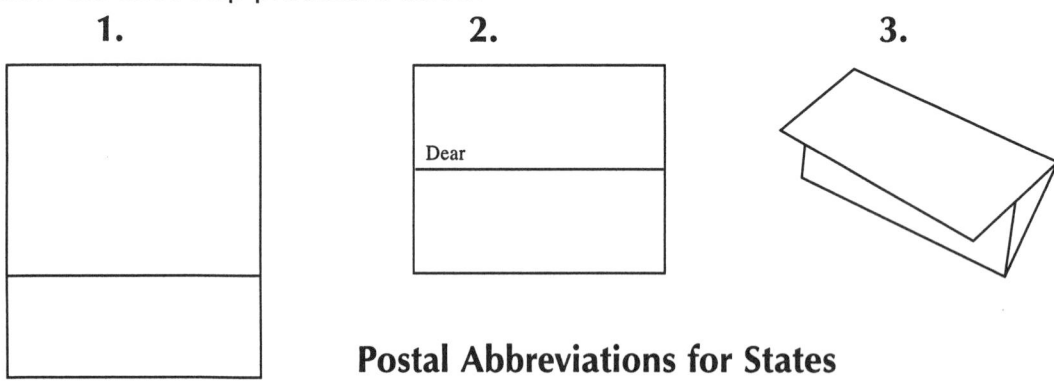

Postal Abbreviations for States

Alabama	AL	Hawaii	HI	Massachusetts	MA	New Mexico	NM	South Dakota	SD
Alaska	AK	Idaho	ID	Michigan	MI	New York	NY	Tennessee	TN
Arizona	AZ	Illinois	IL	Minnesota	MN	North Carolina	NC	Texas	TX
Arkansas	AR	Indiana	IN	Mississippi	MS	North Dakota	ND	Utah	UT
California	CA	Iowa	IA	Missouri	MO	Ohio	OH	Vermont	VT
Colorado	CO	Kansas	KS	Montana	MT	Oklahoma	OK	Virginia	VA
Connecticut	CT	Kentucky	KY	Nebraska	NE	Oregon	OR	Washington	WA
Delaware	DE	Louisiana	LA	Nevada	NV	Pennsylvania	PA	West Virginia	WV
Florida	FL	Maine	ME	New Hampshire	NH	Rhode Island	RI	Wisconsin	WI
Georgia	GA	Maryland	MD	New Jersey	NJ	South Carolina	SC	Wyoming	WY

Name _____

Job Application Cover Letters

As you begin your search of the job market, you will need to know how to write certain job-seeking documents, including an application cover letter, a résumé, and a thank-you letter. Read the following model cover letter and then answer the questions about the writer's purpose below.

2709 N. 3501 Road
Wellington, NE 80544
May 10, 1999

Mr. Stanton White
Personnel Director
The *Daily Times*
PO Box 76
Wellington, NE 80544

Dear Mr. White:

I have just learned from a classified ad in the *Daily Times* that you are seeking a part-time assistant copy editor for summer work in your Wellington plant. I ask that you consider me for this position. I will be 16 on May 28 and will be eligible for a work permit.

As you will see from my résumé, I have work experience that would be useful for this position. I worked for the *Daily Times* in the past as a carrier. I had a paper route for three years, and I received the award for carrier of the month twice during that time. I also have newspaper experience through my job as a reporter for my school newspaper. Mrs. Stephens, the faculty advisor for the school paper, will give me a good recommendation for attendance and punctuality in meeting deadlines. Finally, my career goal is journalism.

My present hobby is photography, and I plan to study journalism and design in college. Working for the *Daily Times* would give me a chance to see what goes on during the production of a newspaper. I will call you next week to see if an interview is possible.

Sincerely,

Robert James

enc.

What does the *enc.* at the end indicate? _____

Who is the audience for this letter? _____

Is the tone formal or informal? _____

What is the writer's purpose? _____

What is the point of paragraph 1?

What is the point of paragraph 2?

What is the point of paragraph 3?

© Instructional Fair • TS Denison   17   IF19304 Writing, Speaking, and Listening

Name _____

Try It!

Find two job ads in the local newspaper (or from another source), and use the information in the ads to fill out the boxes below.

Employer: _____
Address: _____
Position: _____
Skills required: _____
_____

Employer: _____
Address: _____
Position: _____
Skills required: _____
_____

Now choose one of the above job possibilities and, using the information you have written above, draft a cover letter below. Follow the model on the previous page. In addition to the conventions of the standard business letter that you have already learned, remember to "sell" yourself in this letter. Let the person for whom you wish to work know that you are punctual, responsible, interested, and motivated. Finally, be certain that your letter is well organized. Follow the simple outline below, which works for all business letters:

First paragraph: Tell the reader who you are and why you are writing (student seeking a job).
Second paragraph: Explain and support your purpose (why you would do a good job).
Third paragraph: Indicate what you hope or expect to be the next step (an interview).

Name _____

Résumés

Another important job-seeking document is the résumé. Like the cover letter, the résumé is directed to a prospective employer. A good résumé will help you get an interview, which will help you get the job you want. The following model shows you the appropriate information for a young person's entry-level résumé. Study the model and then fill in the résumé worksheet on the next page before you create your own.

ROBERT JAMES
2709 N. 3501 ROAD
WELLINGTON, NE 80544
PHONE: 444-456-2142

OBJECTIVE	Part-time summer position working for local daily newspaper
EDUCATION	Wellington High School, Wellington, NE • Will begin eleventh grade, August 1999 • Maintained "B" average and perfect attendance during last two years

WORK EXPERIENCE	• Raise and sell golden retriever puppies (1998 to present)
	   Ernie James (father), 2709 N. 3501, Wellington, NE 80544
	
	 • Removed and replaced drywall and sheeting (summer, 1999)
	   Mel Howard, Rte 2, Junction, NE 80544
	
	 • Delivered newspapers (1998 to 1999)
	   the *Daily Times,* 100 Quincy, Wellington, NE 80544

SKILLS & PASTIMES	• Photographing local events
	 • Restoring 1956 Ford truck
	 • Playing guitar
	 • Using computer
	   Microsoft Word for Windows 6.0, Adobe PageMaker 6.5
	   Microsoft Works 6.0, Internet/E-Mail

REFERENCES	Mr. Fran Scariot Wellington High School Driver's Ed. Teacher Box 123 (444-433-3252) Wellington, NE 80544 Ms. Barbara Stephens Wellington High School Faculty Advisor Box 123 (444-433-3252) Wellington, NE 80544 Mr. Clint Smith Property Owner Neighbor/Employer 2704 N. 3501 Rd (444-496-9052) Wellington, NE 80544

Name _____

Résumé Worksheet

Complete the following worksheet by supplying personal, school, and work experience (including volunteer work you have done for family or acquaintances).

Name _____
Address _____
Address _____
Phone _____
E-mail _____

OBJECTIVE

EDUCATION

WORK
EXPERIENCE

SKILLS &
PASTIMES

REFERENCES

Try It!

Use a word processor to create your own professional-looking résumé.
Keep it to one page and print it on white or ivory paper (do not try to be "funky" with a résumé).

Have at least two of your peers proofread your résumé and also have one adult proofread it.

A perfect résumé says you are careful in your work—that is an important message!

Interview Follow-Up Letters

It is more than polite to send a thank-you letter after you have been interviewed—it is smart. Consider the following scenario. You own a newspaper. You are hiring an assistant copy editor for the summer. You have interviewed two very impressive teenage applicants who seem equally friendly and qualified, and you are having trouble making up your mind. Then one of them sends you a thank-you letter. The other does not. Which one do you hire?

1901 West 2409 Road
Ottawa, Illinois 61364
April 14, _____

Mr. Warren Pfahl
Managing Editor
Illinois Valley News
420 Second Street
LaSalle, Illinois 61301

Dear Mr. Pfahl:

Thank you for giving me the opportunity to speak with you today about the position of assistant copy editor. I enjoyed talking to you and learning more about this position.

During the tour you gave me, I was very impressed with the size of your plant and the modem technology used throughout every department. I know that I would enjoy working for your newspaper and that I would make good use of my training and experience.

I hope to hear from you soon. In the meantime, I look forward to an opportunity to work for *Illinois Valley News*.

Sincerely,

Karen Parker

Name _____

A thank-you letter should be brief, sincere, and correct. It is one more chance to give the best impression of yourself to someone who may want to hire you. Using the business letter conventions you have already learned, compose a thank-you letter below. Write it to the newspaper owner mentioned on the previous page who has interviewed you for the assistant copy editor's position. Follow the model given.

Name _____

Agendas

Businesses, schools, government agencies, and social clubs usually have formal agendas for their meetings. These agendas reflect the name of the organization; the date, time, and place of the meeting; the schedule of topics in order of presentation; and the names and titles of the people making presentations. List below the clubs and organizations to which you have belonged or currently belong. In the second column, check the clubs or organizations that hold regular meetings. In the third column, check those that follow an agenda.

Clubs/Organizations	Regular Meetings	Use Agenda
_____	_____	_____
_____	_____	_____
_____	_____	_____

Now use the model below to prepare your own agenda for a meeting of one of the organizations you have listed. Use the worksheet on the next page or design your own on a word processor. If you use a computer, follow the suggested conventions listed at the right (point size, for example, may vary). If you create it by hand, approximate the conventions.

Fox River Warriors 4-H

Wedron, Illinois
July 2, 1999
6:30 p.m.

Pledge............................ Sara Spinazola, President

Minutes .... Joe Tuntland, Secretary

Treasury Report .... Jason Kempiak, Treasurer

Project Updates .... Marte Lambert, Project Leader

Correspondence .... Margaret Thompson, Leader

Presentation .... Dawn Geiger, horses

Presentation................. Kathy Barnes, photography

Closing .... Joe Cantlin, Vice President

Refreshments............... Members and Guests

Next Meeting: August 6, 1999

1. Set 1" margins all around.
2. Center organization's name at top (20 pt bold.)
3. Center three different subheadings below it (no abbreviations, correct punctuation, 16 pt bold)—location, date, time
4. Skip four lines; use 14 pt for agenda items.
5. At left margin, type the first agenda item.
6. Next, create a leader, a dotted line like this . . . . that extends to the presenter's name. To create a leader, select tab (under format), set it at 5", and add dotted line.
7. Type the presenter's name and title or topic (use comma between them) after the leader. Repeat steps 5-7 for each of the agenda items.
8. Skip four lines and type and center in 16 pt bold: Next Meeting (add the date)
9. Create a border around the page with drawing and border tools.
10. SPELL CHECK and be certain that the agenda is attractively centered on the page.

© Instructional Fair • TS Denison

Name _____

Try It!

Following the guidelines provided, design an agenda below (or use a word processor) for a meeting or a program.

_____
_____
_____
_____

_____ .... _____
_____ .... _____
_____ .... _____
_____ .... _____
_____ .... _____
_____ .... _____
_____ .... _____

Next Meeting: _____

Name _____

Meeting Notes

Meetings also require note taking. If you ever serve as the secretary of any social club, religious organization, government agency, workplace team, or school board or committee, you will need to know how to take notes, translate them into minutes, and word process them. Minutes are the official record of any organization's proceedings. The agenda is not an official record but the minutes are—they are considered legal documents, and they may be used in a court of law.

The secretary follows a procedure like the one below to keep the minutes organized.
1. Keeps a notebook or ledger for meeting notes only, and dates and signs every entry.
2. Follows the meeting's agenda as an outline for the notes.
3. Divides the notebook pages into two columns—the left for agenda items, the right for notes.
4. Summarizes the main point of discussions and accurately records names, dates, and finances.
5. Records the exact wording of any motions and names of those who moved and seconded.

Assume you are the secretary of the Fox River Warriors 4-H Club. Use the Fox River Warriors' agenda to fill in the left-hand column below. Then on the right-hand side, make up a note for each item on the agenda. Be certain to mention names and reports.

Minutes of the Fox River Warriors' Meeting 7/2/1999	
Pledge 6:30	Sara
Minutes	Approved with corrections.
Treasury Rep.	Bal. of $879.00; July bills paid Aug. bill for $100 for fairground cleanup.
	Respectfully submitted by Joe Tuntland, Secretary

© Instructional Fair • TS Denison

Name _____

Try It!
Use your notes from the previous page to complete the following page of minutes.

REGULAR MEETING OF

_____

TIME AND PLACE   A regular meeting of the _____ was held Wednesday, July _____ in _____.

PLEDGE   The meeting was opened with the pledge led by President

_____

ATTENDANCE   The following officers were present:

_____
_____
_____
_____

APPROVAL OF MINUTES   _____ moved to approve the minutes of the regular meeting held June 6, _____. _____ seconded the motion, which was approved unanimously.

TREASURER'S REPORT   _____ reported a balance of _____
_____
_____
_____
_____
_____

PROJECT REPORTS   _____
_____
_____

© Instructional Fair • TS Denison   IF19304 Writing, Speaking, and Listening

Name _____

Brochures

Clubs, schools, businesses, and other organizations announce, advertise, and solicit with brochures. Attention-getting and informative brochures have the following elements:
- A clearly stated message that includes the essential information: *who, what, when,* and *where*
- An attention-getting headline, picture, and layout (arrangement of words and pictures on page)
- A way for the receiver to contact the sender (business reply form or telephone number)
- A page that is easy and inexpensive to reproduce and distribute (Xerox and mail or hand distribute)

Try It!

The six-panel brochure below is unfinished. Follow the directions on the next page to complete it (or create your own on computer). Cut it out and fold it in thirds as indicated by the dotted lines.

4→ | 3

Fold on line
- -

5→ | 2

- -

6→ | 1

Name _____

1. Decide this brochure's purpose and add the *who, what, when,* and *where* on panel 6.
2. Write a mission statement that expresses the purpose of this organization on panel 2.
3. Add a business-reply form (addressed to the organization) on panel 3.
4. Add a survey on panel 4 (on the back of the business-reply form) for the receiver to fill out.
5. Add your own logo and artwork on panel 5.

**Cut out and fold the brochure
before you write on it to be certain
your layout is correct.**

4
5
6

Name _____

Web Home Pages

If you have Internet access on your computer, you can communicate with the whole world by creating your own Web site. A Web site gives you a presence on the World Wide Web, where people from all over the world can visit you. On your Web site, you can tell visitors about yourself, invite them to write to you, and receive their e-mail. You can also hyperlink (connect) them to some of your favorite Web sites, which they can go to quickly from your site. The first page of a Web site is called a *home page*. On this page and the next, you will practice two basic steps in preparing a home page: planning it and writing the code language. (The final step, actually putting your page on line, will require help from your Internet service provider.)

Step One: Decide what you want on your home page.

Look at the following sample. This author has kept her home page simple, with only one picture, her name, a welcome, and three hyperlinks, which would connect her visitors to her résumé, e-mail, and favorite movie review site. Keep your home page simple so that your visitors can access it quickly. List below six items (pictures, text, and hyperlinks) that you would want on your home page.

Ann McLennan's Home Page

WELCOME!

Hire Me!

My Favorite Movies!

E-Mail Me!

1. _____   4. _____
2. _____   5. _____
3. _____   6. _____

Name _____

Step Two: Plan your page.

Following the model on the previous page, draw a rough draft sketch of your home page on a sheet of paper. Sketch a picture in the upper left. (When you actually design your page, you can use original or computer artwork.) To the right of your artwork, write your name and *Home Page* as a title. Add phrases for two sites to which you want your page hyperlinked. Add an invitation to use your e-mail address (use your real one or make one up). Remember to keep your page simple.

Try It!

Home pages must be written in the Internet's code language, which is called *hypertext mark-up language* (html). Following the model below, write the code for the page you have designed. The code language for your page should be the same as the model's except for your name, your links, and your e-mail address. Notice the *img* instruction in the fifth line; this line instructs the computer to insert the picture from another file. Also the *href* instruction in several places instructs the computer to hyperlink (connect) your visitor to another page or site. The next-to-the-last sentence of the code hyperlinks your visitor to your e-mail site.

```
<html>
<head>
<title>Ann McLennan's Web Site</title>
</head>
<img src="atom.gif" align="left' width="96 height="96" >
<h1> <center>Ann McLennan's Home Page </h1> ></center>
<h3> <center> WELCOME!> <h3> </center>
<h2><p align="LEFT" <a href="resume3.htm">Hire Me! </a> </center>
<p align="CENTER"> <a href="intrest.htm> My Favorite Movies </a>
<p align="RIGHT"> <a href=mail to: armclen1@uiuc.edu">Mail me! </a> </h2>
<html>
```

(Note: h1, h2, and h3 above designate sizes of your text.)

Name _____

Chapter 2: Speaking

Understand Your Audience

Although you may not realize it, you speak many times each day to many different people. Some of your speaking situations are personal (you and one other person), and some are public (you and two or more other people). As with writing, your relationship to your audience is important in deciding not only what you will say but also how you will say it. If your relationship to your audience is personal, you have a great degree of privacy and can often be informal, using incomplete sentences and slang, without fear of offending your audience. If your relationship to your audience is more distant, you will not feel free to use slang or incomplete sentences. The degree of formality changes depending upon how well you know your audience and upon your purpose in speaking to them.

Below place an X in front of the audiences that you would identify as personal and place an O in front of those that you would identify as public. Then circle those you would consider formal.

_____ best friend   _____ salesclerk   _____ school board
_____ members of 4-H   _____ principal   _____ neighbor
_____ librarian   _____ parent   _____ minister

Did you find more personal audiences than public ones? Like most people, your conversations are probably more often personal than public. For example, you almost certainly speak with friends and neighbors more often than with the president of a company or with the mayor of your hometown. To be a truly effective speaker, you will need to be able to adjust what you say to the needs and interests of your audience, whether public or private. To do this you need to learn what your audience knows already, what attitudes your audience has toward the subject, and what interest the audience has in the subject.

Understand Your Purpose

Although the message is the center of any spoken communication, what you say is largely determined by your purpose—why you are speaking. General purposes usually fall into one of three categories—to inform, to persuade, or to entertain—although these purposes often overlap.

Identify each of the following speaking situations as primarily *to inform, to persuade,* or *to entertain.*

_____ 1. to highlight the pleasures of a trip to San Francisco to a senior citizens' group

_____ 2. to explain to your younger brother how to shoot a free throw

_____ 3. to convince your friends to see a particular movie

Name _____

Understand the Speaking Situation

In addition to thinking about your audience and purpose, you need to think about where and how you will deliver your thoughts. Some speaking conventions are culturally determined, such as the distance you will stand from another person or whether you will look directly into another's eyes. Other conventions, such as volume and the use of a microphone, are dictated by the size of the audience. For example, you may be asked to speak to a large group of people for five to ten minutes. This speaking situation may require hours of preparation, several note cards, and some visual aids. On the other hand, you may be seated at a table with a few other people as the chair of a committee meeting. For this speaking situation, your preparation may consist of spending a few minutes to review notes of the last meeting. Before you speak, it is important to find out the size and arrangement of the room, the quality of acoustics, the length of time you are expected to speak, and any specifics the audience expects.

Following are four speaking situations. In the blanks below identify the speaker in the first column, a possible audience in the second column, the purpose in the third column, and, in the last column, whether the situation is formal or informal. The first one has been done for you.

1. Ron enjoys music and would like to learn how to play the guitar. He will call a local store, The Green Tambourine, to inquire about guitar lessons.

2. Sharon is running for president of student council; she will need to give a campaign speech in front of the student body in two weeks.

3. Carlos recently visited Australia and will share his Power Point presentation with a group of friends.

4. Nikki would like to play on the boys' soccer team at school, but the coach told her that girls were not allowed. She plans to pursue the matter with the school administrator.

Speaker	Audience	Purpose	Formal or Informal
Ron	store employee	lessons	informal

In both personal and public speaking situations, you will be more successful if you think about your audience, your purpose, and the speaking situation. In this chapter you will practice strategies to enhance your speaking ability and to give you confidence and experience in both personal and public speaking.

Telephone Communication

Many people spend almost as much time talking to people on the telephone as talking to them face to face. They use the telephone to conduct business, to convey and obtain information, and to visit with family and friends. To make the communication efficient and considerate of others, it is helpful if callers follow some established conventions and rules of etiquette. In general, callers should be prepared to identify themselves, get to the point, and conclude politely. Many recipients appreciate sensitivity to their busy schedules, and everyone values politeness. To develop effective telephone communication skills, practice the conventions below.

Making Telephone Calls

Depending on your relationship to the person you are calling, your approach may be more or less formal. In general, however, have your message prepared ahead of time. Once your call has been answered, you should

- Identify yourself.
- Ask for the person to whom you wish to speak.
- If the person to whom you wish to speak is not available, you may ask if you could leave a message. If that is not possible, ask when the person would be available for you to call back.
- Be certain to say "thank you."

Answering Telephone Calls

The way you answer the telephone depends on where you are. You need to think about what response would be most helpful to the caller.

- If you are at home, your callers know who they called, and a simple "Hello" is appropriate.
- If you are at someone else's home, you would be considerate to answer with that family's name.
- If you work for a business, you would most certainly respond with the name of the company or organization that you represent.

Whenever you answer a call that is not for you, it is polite to ask if you can take a message. If the caller desires to leave a message, you must be certain to do two things: first, get accurate information, including the spelling of the person's name, and write down all details. Second, be certain to deliver the message!

Try It!

Following the conventions for telephone use listed on the previous page and the model on the right, compose a dialogue for one of the occasions below demonstrating appropriate telephone conventions.

- Phone your algebra teacher to tell her that you do not understand the homework assignment.
- Call an 800 number found in a magazine about ordering CDs at 20% off store prices.
- Call the manager of the swimming pool to inquire about hosting a private party for your birthday.
- Phone the city library to reserve the latest best-selling novel.
- Create one of your own.

> Hello, this is John Mays. May I please speak to Mr. Knowles?
>
> This is Bill Knowles.
>
> Hello, Mr. Knowles. I would like to have your permission to be excused from soccer practice this Saturday. Our family has been called out of town.
>
> That is fine, John. I hope it's not an emergency.
>
> No it isn't; my cousin is getting married. Thanks for your understanding. Goodbye.

Now create a possible conversation for one of the occasions below demonstrating appropriate telephone conventions when you are answering the telephone. You will need to add your own information.

- You answer a wrong number when you are at a friend's house.
- You receive a call from your minister asking you to help the youth group serve a meal for the Chamber of Commerce.
- While you are baby-sitting for Mr. Barnard, you take a call from Mr. Barnard's employer who wants him to return the call.
- You take a call for an older sister who is not home. The caller wants you to tell her that her prom dress has arrived and can be tried on for alterations the next day at 2:00 p.m. Your sister is to call back if she cannot make it at 2:00.
- Create one of your own.

With a partner, role-play one of your telephone scripts in front of the class.

If you are bothered by telephone calls soliciting contributions or selling products, talk to your parents about the appropriate response. One effective way is simply to inform the caller that you do not accept these calls at your home. They will usually remove your name from their list.

Name _____

Using Answering Machines

Many people use answering machines to receive calls in their absence. Several guidelines will help you to make the best use of this device.

- Keep the message short, saving time and cost to long-distance callers.
- Be certain the message is not offensive. If your telephone is used for business messages as well as personal communication, songs or jokes are probably inappropriate. You would not want a caller to be annoyed by your phone message.
- Decide what information is most valuable to your caller. Some people identify themselves with a name, some with a phone number, and some with both.
- Conclude the message by stating that you will return the call and asking that the caller leave a short message and a telephone number.

Try It!

Record a message for your own answering machine. Keep your message between 5-10 seconds long. In preparation for making your recording, write your message below. Your teacher may ask you to record your message on a cassette tape.

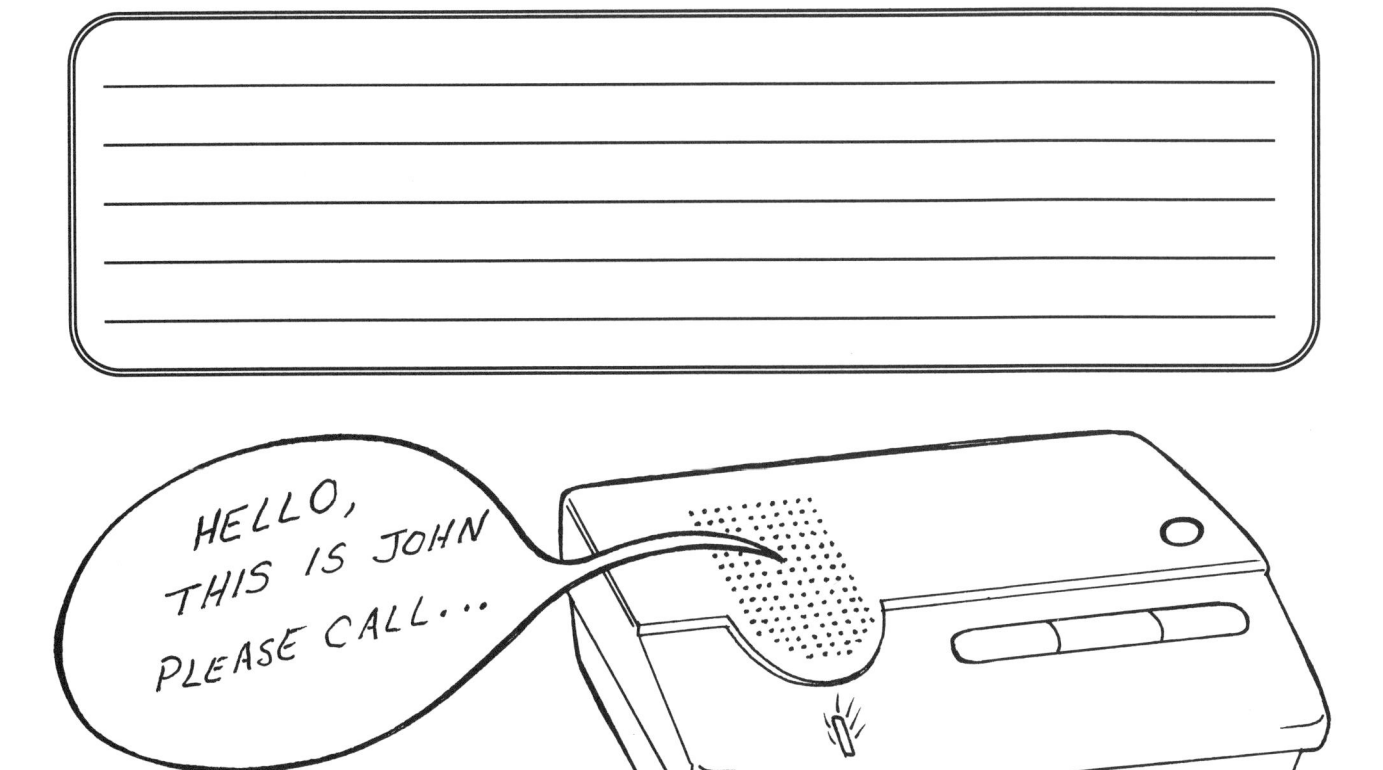

Name _____

Leaving a Telephone Message

Many of the same principles that apply to recording a message apply also to leaving a message. You need to be considerate of the audience—what do they need to know?
- Keep your message short.
- Identify your reason for calling.
- Leave your name and the phone number where you can be reached.

A person's telephone message has its own personality. For example, if your friend has a playful message on the recorder, you may feel comfortable responding with some humor of your own. On the other hand, a businesslike message on an answering machine probably suggests that the person who left that message expects a short, concise message. In this case it would be wise to leave only necessary information.

Try It!

Imagine that you have been ill and are calling your friend to find out the assignments you need to make up for science class. In the box below, write the entire message that you will leave on your friend's answering machine. Your teacher may ask you to record this message on a cassette tape.

_____
_____
_____
_____
_____

Now create scenarios of your own. Place each one on a separate slip of paper and place the slips in a box. After all class members have deposited their slips in the box, draw one and create your message. Your teacher may ask you to record the message on a cassette tape.

© Instructional Fair • TS Denison

Name _____

Requests for Information

Although you may not be aware of it, you probably make requests for information numerous times each day. For example, you may ask for directions, advice, or a thorough explanation of a confusing assignment. Your requests for information may be informal or formal, depending upon how well you know the person to whom you are speaking. If you know the person well, you probably will be rather informal, using his or her first name, a conversational dialogue, and a casual tone. If you do not know the person, you will want to use the appropriate title (Mrs., Miss, Mr., or Dr.), get directly to the point, and avoid slang expressions.

Read the following situations and choose the degree of informality or formality you would use in each request for information. Circle the number on the scale below.

1. the owner of a bicycle shop asking for prices for replacement tires for your dirt bike

    Informal   1   2   3   4   5   Formal

2. your sister's best friend, who is a salesclerk at the local video store, to ask whether the video of the latest movie is available for rental

    Informal   1   2   3   4   5   Formal

3. a professor at the local university who will explain how to use the on-line search engines

    Informal   1   2   3   4   5   Formal

Discuss your responses. Although numbers probably vary, most people will have no problem recognizing that the first situation is less formal than the third.

You may also see that the more formal the situation, the more likely you are to want to prepare ahead of time. However, even in some informal situations, you will want to prepare ahead of time. Before you walk through the door, it is wise to know exactly what your need is and what information you need to provide.

Think of different times when you needed to gain information. List two examples below.

_____

_____

Name _____

Reread the three situations from the previous page. When the person in charge asks, "May I help you?" what do you say? In the blanks below write what each need is and then add a sentence that expresses the need effectively. The first one is done for you.

1. Need __new tires for a mountain bike__

   Effective expression of need: __Yes, I would like two new 26-inch tires for a mountain bike.__
   __The bike is a Mountain Classic XK99, and the tires require 60 pounds of pressure each.__

2. Need _____

   Effective expression of need: _____
   _____

3. Need _____

   Effective expression of need: _____
   _____

Once you know your needs, you are ready to ask for specific information. If you speak to a person who does not know your name, be certain to introduce yourself. Then politely and clearly explain the information that you need. You may follow with specific questions to clarify anything that remains confusing to you.

Try It!

Your teacher will divide the class into pairs. Choose one of the following to role-play in front of the class.

- Ask your language arts teacher for information about entering a poetry contest.
- Ask the sponsor of an organization about club membership requirements.
- Ask your 4-H leader to clarify some points in *Robert's Rules of Order* before your first meeting as president of your local chapter.
- Ask the salesclerk at a music store for suggestions on which CDs to buy for your uncle, who is in his forties and enjoys classic rock and roll music.
- Ask your YMCA league basketball coach to explain the new zone defense that you missed during practice.
- Choose one of your own.

© Instructional Fair • TS Denison

IF19304 Writing, Speaking, and Listening

Complaints

Imagine that you have just purchased a new pair of expensive blue jeans. You get home to find that there are three rather large ink spots on the right leg. What do you do? Circle one or more choices; then discuss your answer with your classmates.

        1) Call a friend and gripe.
        2) Try to get the spots out yourself.
        3) Go back to the store to ask to exchange the jeans.

Probably all three answers were given and, in fact, some people would do all three. Unfortunately, our lives seem to be filled with such events as these, and the above scenario may remind you of similar situations that you have experienced. Fortunately, there are guidelines to help us remedy such situations.

First, be certain that your complaint is legitimate. For example, you would not return jeans you have worn. Second, be timely. If you make your concern known soon after your purchase, your chances of a successful resolution increase greatly. Third, clearly state what the problem is. It often helps to "bury the bad news"—that is, to give some good news (a compliment), state the complaint, and give another bit of good news. This strategy delivers the bad news, the complaint, in such a way that the overall tone remains positive. Finally, tell what you would like done. Remember that effective complaints are determined by both how you speak and what you say.

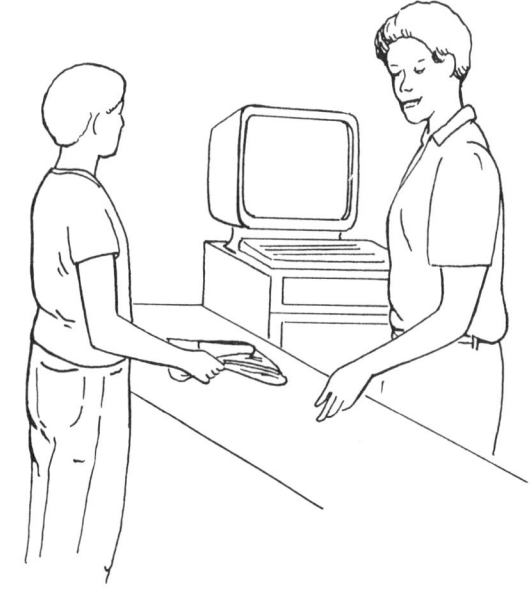

David just purchased a pair of jeans and needs to return them. Read David's complaint and answer the questions that follow on the next page.

> Excuse me, please. I purchased these jeans on sale yesterday and really like the color and style. They fit perfectly. However, my mother noticed that there is a sizeable snag in the right leg. If at all possible, I would like to return them for another pair in the same size and style. I've always had good luck with Class-Act jeans and would like to continue to purchase them. I'd appreciate your help. Thank you.

Name _____

1. What courteous comments appear in the example? List three. _____
   _____

2. What is David's specific complaint (the "bad" news)? _____

3. What are the two items of "good" news that help to put his complaint in a positive light?

   First _____

   Second _____

4. What action does David desire? _____

Besides problems with merchandise, consumers also experience problems with service. In the following example, Mandy has not expressed her complaint effectively.

> Hey! Are you the chic in charge here? Look at my hamburger! I ordered it plain and got ketchup and mustard on it. It's cold, too. I should have known someone would mess up here. My sister always gripes about your bad service. My friends and I are really fed up with this joint.

Revise Mandy's complaint to follow the guidelines on the previous page. Be certain to include what she would probably want the waitress to do to remedy her problem.

_____
_____
_____
_____

Try It!

Create a situation of your own with a partner. Role-play that situation in front of the class. Your classmates will critique each complaint by looking for courteous statements, the specific complaint, the good news that offsets the bad, and the desired remedy.

Solicitations

Have you ever been asked to sell candy bars for a club or organization? If so, you have been asked to solicit. Soliciting often involves selling but may also include asking for permission or asking for a donation. You may ask for permission to use a facility or to borrow equipment for your organization. You may ask for donations—in the form of money or time commitments. All of these requests constitute soliciting.

Successful soliciting can be conducted by telephone or by a face-to-face meeting. The decision to use the phone or to solicit in person usually depends upon your purpose and upon how well you know your audience. If you ask your neighbor to work at a fair booth for an hour, a quick phone call would probably suffice. If you would like a free ton of sand for an outdoor volleyball area to be delivered to the site, a face-to-face meeting with the owner of the sand company would be appropriate. By adjusting what you say and how you say it to correspond with your audience and purpose, you will go far in obtaining positive responses to your solicitations. To ensure a positive response when soliciting, follow the conventions below.

What to Say

- Introduce yourself if you do not know the person well.
- Identify the organization that you represent.
- Say what you are selling or what you would like (a donation of time or money) and how it will benefit your group. If you are soliciting in person and have a brochure or booklet containing pictures and explanations of merchandise, share it with the person.
- Have an order blank or sign-up sheet ready; be prepared with a pen to write up the order.
- Verify that you ordered exactly what the person intended.
- Thank the person for his or her contribution or donation.

How to Say It

- Dress appropriately when soliciting in person.
- Introduce yourself, using a friendly, pleasant voice.
- Speak clearly and avoid speaking too quickly, as many people do when they are nervous.
- Avoid chewing gum—both in person or on the telephone.
- Maintain good eye contact when speaking in person.

Name _____

Read the following solicitations. Would you be more likely to purchase something from Kelly or from Courtney? Why?

> Ah, hi. I'm, ah, Courtney Hoffman. Would ya' like to buy a poster? I've got a lot of rock groups ones. They're for speech club, and I ah gotta' sell at least 50 so I can go to state contest.

> Hello, I'm Kelly Marshall. I'm selling candy bars for our speech club. We are raising money to attend the state speech contest. There are four kinds of bars, and they sell for $1.00 each or six for $5.00. Would you like to buy any?

On the lines below correct the solicitation that you feel needs help.

_____
_____
_____
_____
_____

Try It!

Your teacher will divide you into pairs. Select one of the following situations to role-play. Present your soliciting efforts in front of the class. Vote for the most persuasive "solicitor."

- Your Teens Who Care group would like to have a car wash. You volunteered to ask the city council for permission to have the car wash. You would like to use the city's water at no cost to your organization.
- Your organization would like the minister of a church in town to give the blessing at the yearly banquet. You also would like to use the minister's sound equipment and microphone. It is your job to make these requests.
- Your city league soccer team is in desperate need of new uniforms. If each athlete sells 30 mugs, you will have new uniforms. You are new in town but you start going door-to-door in your neighborhood anyway.
- The middle-school Parent Teacher Organization is selling wrapping paper, cards, and decorations for all kinds of parties. Brightly colored catalogues and order forms are available. Your mother recently accepted a position in management with her company and has no time to solicit. You offer to do it for her.

Your teacher may videotape these.

Name _____

Job Seeking

By the time you graduate from high school, thousands of new jobs will exist. Some of those jobs will require college degrees, some trade school experience, and yet others on-the-job training. All will require an interview. Some interviews may be short and informal, perhaps involving a quick visit with a neighbor to arrange baby-sitting or lawn-mowing services. Others may be long and formal and may involve an office visit with a rigorous question-and-answer session. In either case, interviewing effectively is an important job-seeking skill. The interview provides you the opportunity to emphasize your positive attributes, and good communications skills will help you highlight those positive qualities. Carefully planning what to do before, during, and after the interview will increase your likelihood of securing employment.

Prior to the Interview

Before meeting with a prospective employer, think about your strengths. For example, if you have not missed a day of school, be certain to let the interviewer know. You will be able to highlight your strengths if you know something about the employer—the skills he or she values—and the services or product lines the company offers. Think about the traits your potential employer would like to have in an employee and the skills needed to accomplish the job. Although skills vary from job to job, other desirable personality strengths remain the same. All employers seek employees who demonstrate excellent attendance, a good work ethic, a high-level motivation, and cooperation.

Think about a job you might apply for. Supply evidence that you excel in each of the following areas (evidence may include grade point average, awards, activities, and volunteer work).

attendance/punctuality _____

work ethic _____

motivation _____

cooperation _____

During the Interview

For all interviews, both informal and formal, it is essential that you arrive on time; in fact, it is wise to be a few minutes early. For a formal interview you should be prepared to shake hands and wait for a signal to sit down. Once you are seated and comfortable, the interviewer will begin to ask questions. During the question-and-answer period, you will want to answer each question thoroughly. Your answers should be thoughtful and specific without rambling. If you do not understand a question, you should ask for clarification. By keeping your tone positive, you will convey both a pleasant manner and genuine interest.

Name _____

Nonverbal signals also play an important part in any interview situation. For instance, you can use body language to show that you are interested by leaning forward slightly and by maintaining eye contact. Appropriate dress, which usually means conservative dress, will tell the interviewer that you know how to meet the public. By avoiding an excessive amount of jewelry, heavy cologne, and gum chewing, you send the message that you are aware of appropriate etiquette in the workplace. At the conclusion of the interview, you will want to shake hands.

Below are possible questions an interviewer may ask. Add three of your own.
- What prior work experience do you have?
- What are your strengths?
- What are your weaknesses?
- Why do you want this job?
- What are your qualifications for this job?
- How did you learn about this job?

You will appear prepared and informed if you have questions of your own. Write three questions that you could ask the interviewer below.

_____
_____
_____

After the Interview
Sending a thank-you letter as soon as possible after the interview gives you one more chance to impress a potential employer. If you are still interested in the job, you will want to say that you remain interested in securing employment.

Try It!
Now select a job (some choices appear below). In groups of three each, role-play the interview. One student will assume the role of the employer, the second will play the person being interviewed, and the third will evaluate the interview. Switch positions to enable each group member to play all parts. Your teacher may videotape the interviews.

- baby-sit
- summer day-camp counseling
- snow removal (winter maintenance)
- swimming instruction
- newspaper delivery
- lawn care (summer maintenance)
- swimming pool (locker room attendant)
- recreation aid

On another sheet of paper, develop answers to interview questions.

Introductions

Introducing One Person to Another

One of the pleasures of life is meeting new people. Although introductions usually take less than a minute, they are important. The following conventions will help polish your introductions.

- Introduce younger people to older people. (Mom, this is Erin Jones; she's in my math class.)
- Say both first and last names. When introducing stepparents, it is not only acceptable but also extremely helpful to use last names, especially when the last name of the stepparent is different from the last name of the stepchild (Mrs. Peterson, this is my stepfather, Jeremy Levine.)
- Give some details about each person. This will often get the conversation going. (Amber just moved here from California, where she was on the basketball team. Kelly, didn't you just attend a basketball clinic?)

Introducing Yourself

Probably the most frequent introduction you will make is to introduce yourself to others. The easiest way is simply to say, "Hello, I'm _____." When introducing yourself

- Smile.
- Say your name.
- Provide some detail about yourself that matters to the situation.

Try It!

Using the above conventions, prepare two introductions. Use one of the scenarios below and create one of your own. In some cases you will have to make up names. Write your notes on another sheet of paper.

- Introduce your mother and stepfather to your two friends, Marnie and Erica.
- Introduce your mother and father to your science club sponsor, Mr. Michael Kinman.
- Introduce a new neighbor, Melissa Landers, to your grandfather.
- Introduce your visiting aunt to your minister after Sunday services.
- Introduce a friend from school to a friend from your neighborhood.
- Introduce yourself to a new member of the gymnastics club.
- Your own: _____
  _____
  _____

Name _____

Introducing One Person to a Group

When introducing a speaker to a group, you create a bond between the speaker and audience, and you create interest in the topic. This type of introduction is brief, but it requires advance preparation. Preparation includes acquiring information about both the speaker and the topic.

When you make the introduction, you will probably want to focus first on the topic, telling what the speaker will talk about and giving the exact title of the speech. Second, you will want to tell why the topic will be of interest to the audience. You are then ready to concentrate on the speaker—citing his or her qualifications and highlighting the most important achievements, especially those relevant to the topic. Finally, you will want to give the speaker's first and last name and his or her title. An effective pause before giving the speaker's name and title will direct the audience's attention to the speaker. You may look toward the speaker during the pause, but it is essential that you look at the audience when giving the name. The speaker's name is of utmost importance, and you want the audience to hear it.

Try It!

Using the conventions above for introducing one person to a group and the model to the right, prepare an introduction for one of the occasions below demonstrating effective introductions.

> Tonight's speech is entitled "Internet Use for Teens." Our speaker is the author of several articles on how to use the Internet and publishes a weekly newspaper column on excellent Web sites for teens. She also manages AdamsNet, a multi-county provider of Internet services. I would like to present our speaker—Ms. Camilla Rossi.

- As student council president, introduce a speaker to the student body.
- As president of your 4-H group, introduce a speaker to your group's members.
- As eighth-grade class president, introduce the promotion speaker to family and friends of the graduates.
- As a representative of Teens for Tomorrow, introduce a speaker to members of the middle school Parent Teacher Organization.
- Your own: _____

Name _____

Announcements

Radio announcers tell us that a meeting scheduled for the evening has been canceled due to inclement weather. The school secretary uses the intercom to tell team members about athletic photographs. These are examples of people making announcements. You hear them all the time—you too may be called upon to give them! When you are faced with the task of making an announcement, you can guarantee success by preparing ahead of time.

Organizing the Content

As you prepare, keep in mind that the purpose of an announcement is always the same—to inform. You will want to give factual information covering these categories:

- Who: name of person, club, or organization
- What: event to be held
- When: the day, date, and time
- Where: place (including street address and city)
- Why: reason event is taking place
- Other: essential information, such as items to bring or cost of admission

Label the following announcement by placing *who, what, when, where, why,* and *other* in the blanks to the left of each piece of information.

_____ Youth for Yates City

_____ is sponsoring a car wash

_____ this Saturday, February 26, from 10:00 a.m. to 2:00 p.m. _____ It will be held at the Deluxe Grocers parking lot at 10th and Walnut Streets in Yates City.

_____ the cost of an exterior wash is $4.00 and of an interior and exterior wash is $7.00.

_____ Proceeds will help defray costs of erecting lights at the new Yates City baseball/softball facility.

Name _____

Making the Delivery

If you will read the announcement over an intercom or on the radio, where your audience will hear you but not see you, good oral delivery becomes essential. First, a typed (double spaced) copy will help you read the announcement more easily.

Second, if you speak clearly and naturally, listeners will understand you. To help improve clarity, you can practice reading the announcement aloud. As you practice, you will want to speak loudly enough, pause at punctuation marks, pronounce each syllable, and speak slowly enough. If your audience will see you, you will need to use nonverbal cues as well, such as smiling and standing with erect posture.

Try It!

Create an announcement for one of the following. Read it to your small group. Choose one to read to the class. Your teacher may arrange for certain members of the class to read the school announcements over the intercom as an additional way to practice.

- autumn canned food drive—the homeroom with the most cans per student wins a pizza party
- student council dance
- change in practice time for the volleyball team
- line dance lessons for middle and high school students at the community center on Tuesday and Thursday evening from 6:30 to 8:30
- new youth organization forming; interested members invited
- "The Little Dickens," a preteen literary discussion group, will meet to discuss *A Christmas Carol* by Charles Dickens next Monday at 4:00 p.m. at the city library.
- Your own: _____

Use the following to help you organize your information.

Who? _____
What? _____
When? _____
Where? _____
Why? _____
Other: _____

Name _____

Interviews

When we think of interviews on television or on radio, we think mainly of the person being interviewed. However, the skill of the person conducting the interview is vital to the success of the interview. In fact, viewers and listeners sometimes become loyal fans of the interviewers. For example, think of television interview shows, such as *Larry King Live,* and talk radio interviews, such as those during sports broadcasts. Although these successful interviews look effortless, the apparent ease comes as a result of a considerable amount of work before, during, and even after the interview. Following are six interview strategies. Place a check in front of those that you think are important in conducting an interview.

In an interview situation, would you
- _____ Ask permission to take notes?
- _____ Prepare questions in advance?
- _____ Create open-ended questions?
- _____ Take notes as inconspicuously as possible?
- _____ Think of questions during the interview?
- _____ Ask yes/no questions?

If you checked questions in the first column, you have recognized the importance of careful preparation. If you checked questions in the second column, you also recognized the importance of spontaneity during the interview. Following are some guidelines for preparing and conducting taped interviews.

Before the Interview
- Do some background research about the topic and the person you will interview.
- Analyze the audience who will be receiving the information, concentrating on what they will want to know.
- Prepare questions, limiting those which can be answered with a "yes" or "no" only.
- Contact the person to set up a day and time for the meeting.
- Introduce yourself and tell the person why you desire the interview.
- Ask for permission to take notes or tape record the conversation. (Be prepared to supply your own equipment and make certain that it is in working order.)

During the Interview
- Arrive early, and have all of your materials ready.
- Make certain your clothes are appropriate for the audience who will see your program.
- Be prepared to shake hands when the interviewee arrives.
- Be prepared to listen carefully when the interviewee begins to talk so that you can respond with follow-up questions. Remember, the interview focuses on the person being interviewed, not on you. A good interviewer asks questions (and may paraphrase) but does not insert his or her own opinions or make connections to personal experiences.
- Keep the interview within a reasonable length of time.
- Make eye contact as much as possible.
- Be certain to thank the interviewee at the end of the interview.

Name _____

After the Interview
- Send a follow-up thank-you note to the interviewee.
- If the interview will be published in a newspaper or magazine rather than recorded on tape, read your notes immediately and write your first draft.

Try It!
Interview one of the following.

- new teacher
- coach
- principal
- student of the month
- senior citizen
- long-time area resident
- owner of a new business in town
- your own: _____

Prepare your possible questions below.

_____
_____
_____
_____
_____
_____

Depending on your school's equipment, your teacher may ask you to record your interview on a cassette or video tape rather than writing it. You could even compose an anthology of interviews to share with class members and with other classes.

Discussions

Discussion Groups

You may find discussion groups anywhere a group of people gather to discuss a common interest—in a school setting, in a person's home, or at another meeting place, such as a library or community center. Some groups may designate a member as a leader and another as a recorder, while other groups may prefer all members to exchange their ideas freely. Depending upon the group, both types of discussions can effectively accomplish the group's purpose—to exchange ideas. For instance, a small-group discussion in a language arts class may center upon the exchange of views about the main character in a novel. The sharing of ideas in a civic group may lead members to solve a specific problem, such as the best way to develop recreational use areas within a city.

To be an effective member of a discussion group, you will want to remember the following guidelines.
- Speak loudly enough.
- Express your ideas clearly.
- Avoid interrupting someone who is speaking, and speak one at a time.
- Refrain from laughing at or otherwise offending another group member.
- Stay on topic and share relevant information only.
- Clarify vague points by asking questions or making summarizing statements.

Try It!

Your teacher will separate you into small groups of four to six students. Each group will select a topic from the list below. Groups will discuss this topic for ten minutes while the rest of the class evaluates the discussion, using the six guidelines listed above.
- Cats/dogs make better pets.
- Modern-day heroes are/are not good role models.
- It is better to see an athletic contest in person/on television.
- Professional athletes are/are not paid too much.
- Commercials are/are not a waste of time.
- The book/movie (of the same title) is usually better.
- Your own: _____

After all discussions have been completed, discuss the evaluations in a large-group setting.

Name _____

Committees

Often groups use committees to facilitate business. Committees have specific purposes, such as to decorate or to raise money. Sometimes committee members discuss and then report back to the rest of the group. At other times committee members have the power to do more than discuss; they make decisions—and act upon those decisions. Regardless of its purpose, discussion plays a large role in helping committee members exchange ideas, compromise, and finally agree upon a decision or recommendation.

Committees run smoothly when members do the following:
- designate a chair to guide the discussion
- select a recorder to take notes
- show courtesy as others express their ideas
- stay focused on the purpose of the meeting
- compromise when necessary and support the committee's decision

What kinds of tasks would each of the following committees discuss and carry out?

membership committee: _____

publicity committee: _____

decorating committee: _____

fund-raising committee: _____

Try It!

Your teacher will divide you into committees. Select one person to act as chair and another to act as recorder. Come to an agreement concerning one of the following committee tasks:

- Decorating committee (fall dance): decide what the theme will be, what decorations to purchase, when to decorate, how long it will take, and who will decorate.
- Membership committee: decide how you will recruit new members for the newly formed club (letters, announcements, word of mouth, posters, or a combination of these). Who will perform each task? Where and how will you obtain needed supplies?
- Fund-raising committee: discuss the pros and cons of selling candy bars, having weekly bake sales, selling magazine subscriptions, and having a car wash to raise $500.00 to send two members to a national convention.
- Publicity committee: organize publicity for a literary carnival, which will consist of poetry and prose readings.

Meetings

Nearly everyone attends meetings of some kind. Meetings may consist of a few people, such as weekly student council meetings or meetings of class officers. Meetings may also involve a large number of people, such as 4-H meetings and meetings of the school pep club. Many clubs and organizations, especially those with a large number of members, elect officers who use parliamentary procedure to help the club run smoothly and efficiently.

Below is the order of events that the president or chair follows to conduct the meeting.

Call to Order. The president or chair begins the meeting on time by saying, "The meeting will now come to order."

Minutes. The secretary reads the written business report from the last meeting. The president asks if there are any additions or corrections. If not, members will approve the minutes. If there is a correction, members will approve the minutes as amended.

Treasurer's Report. The treasurer's report includes incoming money and any expenses which were incurred since the last meeting. The report ends with the current balance.

Committee Reports. The president asks each committee chair for a report. Chairs read their reports. If a chair has no report, he or she will say, "I have no report."

Unfinished Business. Members will discuss business that was begun at an earlier meeting.

New Business. Members will bring up new business. Discussion will follow with perhaps the forming of committees to explore the new issues.

Announcements. The president asks for announcements.

Guest Speaker. Some organizations invite a guest speaker to present a program.

Adjournment. The president ends the meeting by asking for a motion to adjourn. A member says, "I move to adjourn the meeting." Another member seconds the motion by saying, "I second the motion." The president announces that the meeting is adjourned.

Try It!

Attend a school board, 4-H, city council, or another meeting in your town. Take notes on the group's business meeting. How closely did the group adhere to parliamentary procedure? Report back to the class and evaluate the meeting.

Name _____

Below are statements taken from a club meeting. Some of the statements do not follow parliamentary procedure or are not appropriate for a large-group meeting. Circle YES if the statement follows the guidelines of parliamentary procedure. Circle NO if it breaks etiquette of parliamentary procedure. Rewrite the NO statements so that they follow protocol.

YES   NO   "Come on, guys! Be quiet! It's 4:00 p.m. and time to get started if we want to get out of here at a decent time."

YES   NO   "The meeting of Youth for Action will come to order."

YES   NO   "Sarah, will you please read the minutes of our last meeting?"

YES   NO   "Hey, I don't agree with what she said about the last meeting."

YES   NO   "I would like to amend the minutes to read 'five members attended the Volunteers for Action in Small Communities' rather than four members as was read in the minutes."

YES   NO   "I second that motion."

Corrections

_____

_____

Try It!

Divide the class into two groups. Role-play a club meeting. Create a club name, elect (or assign) officers, and conduct a "monthly" meeting. Your teacher may require the secretary, treasurer, and all committee chairs to hand in reports. Meetings may be videotaped and evaluated to determine how closely each adheres to parliamentary procedure.

Name _____

Speeches

Does the thought of speaking to a large group of people make you nervous? If your answer to that question is "yes," you are among the majority of people. Many people fear speaking to large groups; in fact, most people list giving speeches as their number-one fear! This fear often results from the fact that speaking to large groups usually involves unfamiliar people and equipment. For instance, in a formal speaking situation, the speaker most often uses a microphone and probably does not know most of the members of the audience. However, the speaker does know ahead of time when the speech will occur and how long he or she will speak, giving the speaker ample time to prepare. Effective preparation involves understanding your audience, topic, and purpose; planning your speech; and practicing your delivery.

Understanding Your Audience, Topic, and Purpose

Speaking to large groups requires many of the same skills as writing a good essay. First you will want to consider your audience by selecting a topic that is appropriate as well as interesting to them. You will also want to establish your purpose—to inform, persuade, or entertain—and keep your purpose in mind as you research your topic.

Supply the speaker, audience, topic, or purpose for these speaking situations. The first one has been done for you. Remember, audience, topic, and purpose go hand-in-hand—one determines the other.

Speaker	Audience	Topic	Purpose
middle school basketball coach	school board	new uniforms	to persuade
high school counselor		class schedules for freshman year	
middle school student	peers who may be interested in joining Volunteens, a new civic organization		
member of the community theater			
	first-grade children		to entertain
		rock collection	

© Instructional Fair • TS Denison   55   IF19304 Writing, Speaking, and Listening

Name _____

Planning Your Speech

Like good writers, good speakers keep the audience in mind as they prepare a speech. Not only should the information interest the audience, but the organization should be easy to follow. The best way to serve your audience is to organize your thoughts into a predictable order, using an introduction, a body, and a conclusion.

The Introduction. The introduction should state what your speech will be about (the topic) and what you hope to accomplish (the purpose). It sets up certain expectations for the audience, which should be met with the remainder of the speech. Effective introductions capture the attention of the audience by using strategies such as asking a question, telling a humorous or interesting anecdote, or giving a startling fact or statistic.

Imagine that you are giving a speech about the benefits of regular exercise. Think of introductory sentences using each of the following attention-getting devices.

Fact or Statistic: _____

Question: _____

Anecdote: _____

The Body. The body of your speech usually has several parts—one for each main idea. Each main idea should have its own paragraph(s), and each paragraph should stick to a single idea. Finally, all ideas should be arranged in a predictable order, such as chronological order, order of importance, or spatial order. Signal words, such as *first, next, finally, most important, then, next to,* and *as a result* help your audience to follow your ideas.

What main ideas would you want to explore if you were to give the speech on exercise?

_____   _____

_____   _____

The Conclusion. The conclusion lets your audience know that you are finished. Effective conclusions reinforce the main ideas of the speech and let the audience know what the speaker expects them to do next. For example, in the conclusion of a persuasive speech, you may ask the audience to buy a product, contribute to a worthy cause, or try a new hobby. You will want a powerful last sentence—and it should be the *last* sentence. A common mistake beginners make is concluding twice! To avoid this potential problem, you should refrain from adding "That's it" or "That's all I have." Such words reduce the effectiveness of any conclusion.

Write one sentence which effectively concludes the speech on exercise.

Name _____

Practicing Your Delivery

Note Cards. Note cards keep a speaker organized. They serve as guideposts for remembering all important points. When preparing your note cards, you will want to write neatly, putting one or two ideas on each card. If your speech contains material that you wish to give word for word, you may find it necessary to write out those sentences. Upon finishing all your note cards, it is a good idea to number them. Numbering will allow you to organize your information quickly should the note cards become mixed up.

Although you may wish to write your introductory sentence on a note card, it is wise to refrain from writing out the entire speech word for word. You will want to glance at the card and be able to talk from those notes. Speaking from notes ensures a more natural delivery.

Oral Delivery. Good oral delivery is essential when giving a speech. You will want to consider your rate of speech, your volume, and your pitch. Silence—the use of effective pauses—also plays an important role in producing an effective speech.

Nonverbal messages also contribute to a successful speech. Posture, dress, eye contact, and gestures work together to present an impression. You will want to stand straight, maintain eye contact, use natural hand gestures, and dress appropriately. It is a good idea to dress slightly more formally than you think the audience will be dressed.

Select a poem or short prose piece. Real it aloud several times, varying your rate, volume, and pitch each time. Pause at different places. Use the following checklists as an evaluation tool as you practice. You may want to practice by speaking in front of a mirror, by speaking into a tape recorder, or even by videotaping yourself. As you evaluate, place yourself in the role of your audience. You may want to ask a friend or family member to evaluate you.

Voice

_____ appropriate volume

_____ normal speaking rate

_____ varied tone

_____ avoidance of "fillers" (*ah, er, um*)

Appearance

_____ erect posture

_____ appropriate clothing

_____ natural gestures

_____ good eye contact

_____ pleasant facial expressions

© Instructional Fair • TS Denison

IF19304 Writing, Speaking, and Listening

Name _____

Try It!

Use the chart below to organize your speech, using at least two main points and as many as four if appropriate.

Topic:		
Purpose:		
Audience:		
Introduction:		
Body:		
Main Point:	Main Point:	Main Point:
Detail:	Detail:	Detail:
Detail:	Detail:	Detail:
Detail:	Detail:	Detail:
Conclusion:		

Name _____

Campaigns

For school and civic organizations to run smoothly and efficiently, they need officers who can help them to meet their goals while accommodating members' busy schedules. Members of these organizations elect candidates they feel show the best potential for carrying out the duties of the office. Very often, officers are required to campaign for these positions, highlighting their qualifications for office.

Along with remembering the verbal and nonverbal conventions of giving a speech, you will find the following guidelines important in organizing your campaign speech.
- State your name.
- State the office for which you are running.
- Describe your qualifications.
- Describe your goals for the group.
- Ask for members of the audience to vote for you.
- Repeat key ideas.
- End with a memorable or catchy slogan.

Read the following example of a campaign speech. Using the information in the example, fill in the requested information on the next page.

> Hello! My name is Paul McAndrew and I'm running for the office of President of Active Teens. I have been a member of Active Teens for four years and have held several positions of leadership in the club during the past three years, including being chair of the fund-raising committee, which brought in over $500.00, and chair of the membership committee for the past two years. I'm happy to say that membership has grown by 15% during this time period.
>
> My goals as president include 1) continuing our fund-raising efforts to contribute to the new city recreation center, 2) more educational field trips, and 3) more monthly activities. Finally, I would like to see us begin an after-school volunteer program which will provide children in grades 1 through 3 with supervised activities from 3:00 to 5:00 p.m. May I count on your vote in Tuesday's election? Remember—we need continued fund-raising, field trips, and monthly activities. A vote for Paul McAndrew is a vote for progress!

Name _____

Name: _____ Office: _____

Qualifications: _____

Goals: _____

Ask for vote: _____

Repetition of key ideas: _____, _____, _____

Catchy slogan: _____

In a campaign speech your charisma—or the way you present yourself—is as important as what you say. Enthusiasm goes a long way in impressing your audience. It is also a good idea to follow etiquette and avoid criticizing your opponent; you will earn more votes by focusing on the things you will strive to accomplish if you are elected.

Try It!

Assume that you are running for one of the following offices and write your campaign speech. Use the space below to organize your notes.

- President of student council
- Vice-president of your class
- Secretary of community theater group
- Treasurer of church group
- Sergeant at Arms (or parliamentarian) of Leaders of Tomorrow Club

Name/introduction: _____

Office: _____

Qualifications: _____

Goals if elected: _____

_____

Ask for vote: _____

_____

Repetition (summary) of key ideas: _____

Catchy slogan: _____

Name _____

Honors

Honors play an important part in people's lives. Everyone enjoys being recognized for personal achievements—whether it be for hours of volunteer work, for perfect attendance at school, for selling the most Girl Scout cookies, or for achieving an academic or sports honor. You may sometimes find yourself in the position to receive an award or to give an award. In either situation, certain guidelines will help you get through the event with poise and confidence.

Receiving an Honor

Making a good impression when accepting an award shows the audience that you are truly deserving of the honor. In many instances, especially when a large number of people will receive awards, it is proper to simply accept the award, shake hands (receive the award or certificate with your left hand and shake with your right hand), and say "thank you." In other situations, you may be expected to say a few words. As always, appropriate dress plays an important part, and in some cases it becomes extremely important. For example, high heels may present a problem if steps lead to the platform.

If you know ahead of time that you will receive the award and that acceptance remarks from you will be expected, advance preparation will help you make that good impression. The following guidelines will help you organize what to do and say when receiving an award.

- Shake hands.
- Accept the award.
- Thank the person giving the award.
- Tell the audience that you are honored.
- Explain why the award is meaningful.
- Thank the audience.

Try It!

Imagine that you will receive one of the following awards. On the lines below, briefly outline what you will say. Be ready to give your acceptance speech to the class. You may wish to coordinate your efforts with a student who will present you with your award.
- an award for the most improved summer soccer league player
- a service award for volunteer hours spent reading to children at the library and to senior citizens at the local nursing home
- the American Legion Award for good citizenship
- an award for being the outstanding student in your school

Statement of thanks: _____

Statement that you are honored: _____

Statement describing the importance of the honor: _____

© Instructional Fair • TS Denison

Name _____

Presenting an Honor

When you are asked to present an award, you are placed in a position of recognition along with the person being honored. Nevertheless, you will want to remember to focus on the person receiving the award and not on yourself. Since awards celebrate achievement, you will want to determine what you want to say and practice ahead of time. As you practice the presentation, you will want to be certain that you sound sincere. Presenters of awards generally observe the following conventions:

- Tell what the award is.
- Give the criteria for it.
- Tell what the recipient accomplished.
- State the full name of the recipient.
- Give the award while shaking hands with the recipient.

Try It!

Using the above conventions and the model to the right, present one of the following awards. Use the lines below to plan your notes.

- As student council president, present the outstanding student award based on scholarship, leadership, and service.
- On behalf of a civic organization, present a service award at the annual mother/daughter or father/son banquet.
- As captain of an athletic team, give the most improved trophy, an award voted upon by fellow team members.

> It is my pleasure to give this year's Community Service Award for Teens. To qualify for this award, a teen must reside in our county, be between the ages of 13 and 18, and give at least 100 hours of time to three or more service projects. This year's recipient has spent over 150 hours in work with scouts, senior citizens, and the recreation program. It is an honor to give this year's service award to Ryan Fogel.

Honor: _____ Criteria: _____

Winner's Accomplishments: _____

_____

Name of Winner: _____

© Instructional Fair • TS Denison

IF19304 Writing, Speaking, and Listening

Name _____

Chapter 3: Listening

Hearing Sounds Around You

Listening is an activity whose importance often goes unrecognized. We listen to learn new things, and we listen for enjoyment. In fact, we spend far more time listening than writing, reading, or even speaking, but rarely do we think about learning how to listen better. Because listening is so important, we need to learn strategies for making our listening more effective. Before reading further, stop a moment and listen for the sounds around you. List every sound that you hear.

_____   _____   _____

_____   _____   _____

_____   _____   _____

You were probably surprised at the number of sounds that you could identify. Much of the time you are not aware of many of these sounds, but you are hearing them anyway. Unlike speaking and writing, which occur only when you choose to do them, your hearing mechanism is never turned off, even though it may sometimes be "tuned out." Look over the list below and place a check mark beside those sounds that you hear on a daily basis.

____ teacher's voice	____ car horn	____ bird's chirp
____ parent's voice	____ TV program	____ police siren
____ friend's voice	____ radio program	____ alarm clock
____ floor creaking	____ train whistle	____ telephone ring
____ water running	____ car engine	____ computer beep
____ bells	____ dog's bark	____ appliance motor
____ stereo	____ children playing	____ other _____

Now circle the sounds that you usually listen to intently. Compare your responses with those of class members. Which ones did most people check? Which ones did they circle? Probably you found that you listen intently to fewer than half of the sounds you hear. This happens because you tend to listen carefully only when you have some reason for doing so.

© Instructional Fair • TS Denison   63   IF19304 Writing, Speaking, and Listening

Name _____

Dealing with Distractions

Even in situations where you want to listen intently, you may not be as effective as you could be. Distractions, discomfort, and lack of background all influence your ability to pay close attention. Check your listening habits by placing an "x" in the appropriate places below.

Types of Distractions	Often	Occasionally	Rarely
1. I find myself daydreaming when people are talking.			
2. I have to ask for instructions to be repeated.			
3. I am distracted by a speaker's appearance or mannerisms, missing what is being said.			
4. I have difficulty listening to people with whom I strongly disagree.			
5. I find it difficult to listen closely when the material seems too difficult.			
6. I forget the names of people who have just been introduced to me.			
7. I tend to miss the beginning words of a speaker.			
8. I try to listen to two things at once.			
9. I find myself thinking of what I will say next when someone else is speaking.			
10. I have difficulty paying attention when I'm tired or uncomfortable.			

If you are like most people, you had most checks in the "Often" and "Occasionally" columns, reflecting the fact that your mind is constantly distracted by various sources both external and internal. In order to listen successfully, you need to be able to block out some of these competing sounds and thoughts. The activities in this chapter will help you to better understand the difficulties listeners face and suggest some strategies for overcoming them.

Name _____

Listening With Purpose

When you pick up a favorite magazine, you rarely begin on page one and continue to the end. More than likely you thumb through the magazine or scan the table of contents, then make your selection based on what interests you. The same thing happens with listeners. They tune speakers in or out depending on their interest.

List below three topics that would interest you if you were to hear a presentation—either on radio or television, or in person. Following each topic, describe the kinds of information you would hope to hear.

Topic #1 _____

_____

Topic #2 _____

_____

Topic #3 _____

_____

Now list three topics that would definitely bore you.

Topic #1 _____

Topic #2 _____

Topic #3 _____

Compare your choices with those of your classmates. On the board, make a master list of all topics identified. Beside each topic, list the total number of people in the class who would find it interesting and the number who would find it uninteresting. What your lists will probably show is a wide variety of distinct tastes. Your interests enable you to listen attentively.

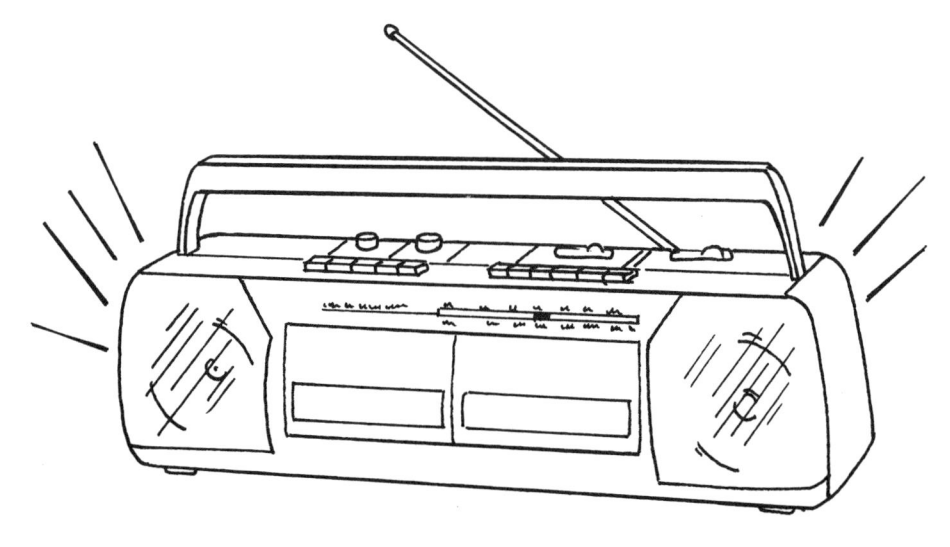

Name _____

In addition to choosing different topics, listeners have different purposes for listening. People listen for pleasure, to gain information, or to evaluate the truth or worth of a speaker's message. Think of a time when you listen for each of these reasons:

Pleasure _____

Information _____

Evaluation _____

If you were to listen to the four speakers listed below, how interested would you be, and why would you be interested? In the blanks below, identify your probable responses. In the first column write "Very Interested," "Mildly Interested," or "Tuned Out." In the second column, identify your purpose for listening as "Pleasure," "Information," "Evaluation," or "Not Interested."

Speaker and Occasion	Speaker's Purpose	Your Interest Level: *Very Interested Mildly Interested Tuned Out*	Reason for Your Interest: *Pleasure Information Evaluation*
Golfing coach talking to school golf team	To give tips on use of new titanium clubs		
Teacher talking to computer writing class	To demonstrate use of graphics software		
Retirement property representative on television	To sell property in a retirement community		
Music video on television music channel	To boost ratings and sell music videos		
Presidential assistant on radio explaining proposed tax changes	To convince the public to support the president's policy		
Siskell and Ebert speaking on TV program, *At the Movies*	To review current movies and make recommendations		

© Instructional Fair • TS Denison

IF19304 Writing, Speaking, and Listening

Name _____

Reading Body Language

When you listen to someone speak, you not only listen to the words they say, but you also "read" their body language. In the first column below are some common gestures of speakers and, in the second column, some possible messages. In small groups select one person to demonstrate each gesture, with group members identifying possible messages. Items in the second column can be used more than once. Compare your group's responses with those of other groups.

Speaker's Gesture	**Possible Message**
____ 1. Makes eye contact with audience	a) speaker is nervous
____ 2. Rolls, crumples, and twists notes	b) speaker is confident
____ 3. Talks rapidly	c) speaker is suggesting caution
____ 4. Paces forward and backward	d) speaker wants to create emphasis
____ 5. Stands stiffly and rigidly	e) speaker is asking for silence
____ 6. Puts palms up	f) suggests giving or receiving an idea
____ 7. Puts palms down	g) suggests rejecting an idea
____ 8. Puts palms diagonal, about shoulder high	h) suggests closeness with the audience
____ 9. Makes clenched fist	i) speaker is challenging audience
____ 10. Winks	
____ 11. Puts finger to the lips	
____ 12. Balances weight comfortably on both feet	
____ 13. Stands with weight shifted onto one foot	
____ 14. Points with the index finger	
____ 15. Exits quickly	

To practice reading a speaker's body language, write the following situations on slips of paper. Each person chooses a situation out of a hat and acts it out. Audience members write down the "messages" that they receive.

telephone call	singing	skating
writing a letter	studying	changing a tire
gossip	fishing	hitchhiking
puppet show	bowling	arguing
driving a car	boxing	putting on shoes

© Instructional Fair • TS Denison

IF19304 Writing, Speaking, and Listening

Name _____

Listening Actively

Although listening is largely a mental activity, it is also a physical activity. Below is a list of strategies for making yourself a more attentive listener. Place a check beside those strategies that you customarily use when listening to someone speak. Circle those that you need to work on.

_____ Sit up straight.

_____ Lean forward.

_____ Look at the speaker.

_____ Nod head in agreement.

_____ Take notes.

_____ Listen for title and write it down.

_____ Create headings and subheadings in notes, concentrating on main ideas rather than details.

_____ Underline key ideas in your notes.

_____ Draw pictures representing the speaker's ideas.

_____ Summarize the speaker's ideas periodically, keeping the main purpose in mind.

_____ Construct questions.

_____ Try to predict the speaker's next point.

_____ Make connections between what you hear and what you already know from your own experience.

_____ Keep an open mind. Don't argue with the speaker in your mind, shutting off possible points of agreement.

_____ On the other hand, listen critically. Don't allow yourself to agree too readily.

_____ Be aware of manipulative speakers.

_____ Be aware of other listeners' responses.

_____ Try to read the speaker's body language.

_____ Try not to be distracted by unintended mannerisms of the speaker.

_____ When your mind wanders, force concentration by taking more notes.

_____ If a distracting thought keeps recurring, make a note of it so you can forget it for now and return to it later.

Directions and Messages

How often do you find yourself listening as someone is giving directions and, as soon as the speaker has finished, turning to the person next to you to ask, "What are we supposed to do?" In fact, many times a day we are called on to take directions or messages of some kind, and very frequently we end up without necessary information. Although some of the difficulty may be the speaker's fault, often we have not been fully attentive. For example, sometimes it takes us a minute or two to settle down to listen. Unfortunately, those first moments are often when critical information is given.

Following Directions

The following exercise will help you to practice your listening skills by visualizing what a speaker is saying and listening for cue words. Repeat the activity until each person in the group has had practice giving and receiving directions.

1. Create groups of three, numbering the people in each group "one," "two," and "three." Persons one and two in each group arrange their desks so that they are sitting back to back. Person three sits nearby, close enough to hear what the other two say.

2. Person one draws an original diagram, taking care not to let person two see it. Person one describes the diagram to person two, who attempts to reproduce the diagram without seeing it or asking any questions.

3. Person three writes down what person one says, noting in particular signal words such as "first," "second," "then," etc.

4. When person two has completed the diagram, persons one and two compare diagrams. All three members of the group analyze the instructions, discussing strengths and weaknesses in giving directions and listening to them.

Here is another exercise that uses visualization in following directions.
1. Each person writes down the route a person would follow to get from the school to some public building or store.
2. As each person reads the directions to the class, class members identify the building.
3. As a large group, list on the board the signals that aided in communication. What, if anything, hindered communication?

Taking Telephone Messages

Taking messages, either for yourself or for others, is an important listening activity. Getting incomplete or inaccurate information can be frustrating and sometimes serious. Often these messages are given over the telephone, either in person or on answering machines. A careful listener knows what information to look for and what questions to ask if the information is not provided.

In most cases a person leaving a message provides the following information:

- The caller's name
- The necessary information (who, why, what, when, where, how, etc.)
- The number where the caller can be reached

For example, assume that the service department of the Acme Motor Company called to speak to Ms. Suseela Rani. Finding that she was not home, the caller left the message below. Select one person to read the message aloud, while the rest of the class takes notes to give to Ms. Rani. On the next page write the message you would leave for Ms. Rani.

> *This is the service department of the Acme Motor Company calling. Would you please tell Ms. Rani that the repairs she requested on her car are completed, but we've found a problem with the brakes. Our service department will be working only half a day tomorrow, so she needs to get back to us today if she wants the brakes repaired before Monday. Have her call 333-0000 and ask for Pat.*

Name _____

Using your notes, write the message you would leave for Ms. Suseela Rani:

[ ]

Compare information with classmates.
- Who is the caller?
- What is the important information?
- At what number can the caller be reached?

Try It!

Working in small groups, write individual messages to read to the rest of your group. Be certain to include all necessary information.

[ ]

When everyone has completed writing their messages, take turns reading them to the rest of the group. Listeners should take notes, identifying the following information:

- Who is the caller?
- What is the important information?
- At what number can the caller be reached?

Name _____

If you are taking a message in which necessary information is omitted, you need to ask for that information. For example, assume a local bookstore called to give your brother this message:

> *Would you please tell Mr. McLennan that the book he ordered is in and can be picked up anytime this week between 9 and 5? We will keep the book for one week. If it is not picked up, we will return it to the supplier. The cost is $13.80.*

What two pieces of information should you ask for before hanging up the phone?

1. _____

2. _____

You probably identified the missing information as the name of the caller and the telephone number. In this case, it may not be absolutely necessary to know the caller's name, but if your brother were unable to pick up the book for several days and the store had a large staff, it would be helpful for him to speak to the person most familiar with the order. Also, your brother may be able to find the store's telephone number in the telephone book, but it would be much more convenient to have it immediately available.

Try it!

Again working in small groups, have each person create a message to give to the rest of the group. This time, instead of including all necessary information, leave out some part that the listener would need to have. As each person reads his or her message, group members should ask for the missing information. Write your incomplete message in the space below.

One-on-One Conversation

Have you ever found yourself in a conversation with someone and it seemed as though the other person would never let you speak? When you did get a chance to speak, did it seem that the other person did not really listen, but was just waiting for a turn to talk again? We all do this at times, of course, but conversations are most productive and most enjoyable when both people listen with interest and an open mind.

Practicing Empathetic Listening

One way to be a good listener is to try to understand the other person's point of view by asking questions and restating the other person's position. Below are two passages in which people disagree on some issue. Working in pairs, have one person read the passage and read the response instruction. The second person responds to the passage as an empathetic listener—that is, a listener who tries to understand. Take turns reading the statements and responding to the passages by restating the speaker's position before further explaining your view. (The first response is done for you, but try it yourself first; then compare it with the model.)

Passage 1: One person reads aloud while others listen.

Mary: Ernie, I think we should have the school car wash in the city park this year.

Ernie: I don't know why you always want to have the car wash in the city park instead of the mall. There's nowhere for people to go while they wait for their cars to be washed. Also, the mall is a lot closer to the school. Kids who have band practice in the morning can walk from the school to the mall, so we'll have more help. Maybe people who are at the mall shopping would see us and stop by to have their car washed. They're not going to be out driving around the park.

Listener's Response
Pretend that you are Mary. How would you restate Ernie's position to show that you have listened with an open mind and tried to understand his view?

> Ernie, I see your point that people could shop while their cars are being washed, and I'm sure you're right that we would get some customers from shoppers. Maybe we could even get some band students to help us. I thought the park would be good because of the water supply, which we've had trouble with in the past. Also, safety might be a problem. If the mall is busy, we would have students out walking around in the middle of traffic. Maybe we could ask whether the mall could provide water and a roped-off area and, if not, go to the park. What do you think?

Name _____

Passage 2: One person reads aloud while others listen.

Debbie: Mike, can I borrow your book on the Anasazi people of Arizona?

Mike: I can't believe you're asking me this. People in this house are always taking my things. They borrow my tapes, use my radio, eat my favorite cereal, mess up my tools, and never put anything back where it belongs. I'm going to put a lock on my door to keep people out of my room. If anyone wants to borrow anything, they'll have to ask me. But I can tell you right now, the answer will be "no" until I see that people around here start respecting my property.

Listener's Response:
If you were Debbie, how would you restate Mike's position to show that you understood?

_____
_____
_____
_____
_____

Sometimes being an empathetic listener means that you try to do something to help. At other times, simply *listening* may be all you can do. Below are two passages from Willa Cather's *O Pioneers!*—a novel about the hardships of early American immigrants. In each passage a character has a problem. Working in pairs, have one person read the passage and the response questions. The second person responds to the questions as an empathetic listener. Take turns reading the statements and responding to questions.

Passage 3: One person reads aloud while others listen.

On the sidewalk in front of one of the stores sat a little Swede boy, crying bitterly. He was about five years old. . . . He cried quietly, and the few people who hurried by did not notice him. He was afraid to stop anyone, afraid to go into the store and ask for help, so he sat wringing his long sleeves and looking up a telegraph pole beside him whimpering, "My kitten, oh, my kitten! Her will freeze!"

[The child's sister] did not notice the little boy until he pulled her by the coat. Then she stopped short and stooped down to wipe his wet face.

"Why, Emil! I told you to stay in the store and not to come out. What is the matter with you?"

"My kitten, sister, my kitten! A man put her out, and a dog chased her up there." His forefinger, projecting from the sleeve of his coat, pointed up to the wretched little creature on the pole.

© Instructional Fair • TS Denison

Listener's Response
1. What is the situation?
2. If you were the sister, how would you show that you understood?

_____
_____
_____
_____
_____

Passage 4: One person reads aloud while others listen.

"[The doctor] is coming over tomorrow. But he says father can't get better; can't get well." The girl's lip trembled. She looked fixedly up the bleak street as if she were gathering her strength to face something, as if she were trying with all her might to grasp a situation which, no matter how painful, must be met and dealt with somehow . . . .

Carl did not say anything, but she felt his sympathy . . . . The two friends stood for a few moments on the windy street corner, not speaking a word, as two travelers, who have lost their way, sometimes stand and admit their perplexity in silence.

Listener's Response
1. What is the situation?
2. If you were Carl, what would you do to show that you understood?

_____
_____
_____
_____
_____

Name _____

Conducting Interviews

Interviews are a special type of one-on-one conversation in which the interviewer gets to know a great deal of information about the person being interviewed. Listening intently and asking appropriate questions are critical skills. Interview a family member about some family legend—a story of hardship, adventure, accomplishment, or tradition. In conducting your interview, follow these steps:

1. Construct questions to ask during the interview using *who, what, why, when, where,* and *how* questions.
2. Listen closely to the speaker's answers, taking notes of important information.
3. Encourage the speaker to offer information that goes beyond your questions.
4. As the speaker talks, jot down additional questions that occur to you.
5. Write up your notes. (You may want to check the accuracy with the person you interviewed.)
6. Share your family legend with the class.
7. As class members listen, they should write down at least two questions for each presenter to answer.

My Family Legend

A story of _____

By _____

Name _____

Group Discussion

As difficult as it is to really understand one another in a one-on-one conversation, it is even more difficult with a larger group. Interruptions are especially a problem as more ideas come into the discussion. Although it is natural to want to interrupt when others are speaking—in fact, it is a sign of your engagement in the conversation—everyone learns more when speakers complete their thoughts and listeners wait their turn.

Creating Full Group Participation

In small groups, select one member to read aloud each of the following Chinese fables. The audience members should take notes and formulate topics or questions for discussion. After reading each fable, the reader will monitor the discussion, recording the number of times each audience member participates in the discussion. Each audience member will be responsible for at least one contribution from the following list for each fable:

(1) asking a discussion question (question that cannot be answered with a right/wrong or yes/no answer),
(2) pointing out a possible theme relating to human behavior,
(3) describing some personal experience with a similar behavior,
(4) identifying words or ideas that specifically reflect the Chinese culture,
(5) sharing an original illustration depicting something in the fable.

Fable 1: One person reads aloud while others listen.

Suspicion
Li Zi

A man who lost his axe suspected his neighbor's son of stealing it. He watched the way the lad walked—exactly like a thief. He watched the boy's expression—it was that of a thief. He watched the way he talked—just like a thief. In short, all his gestures and actions proclaimed him guilty of theft. But later he found his axe himself when he went out to dig. And after that, when he saw his neighbor's son, all the lad's gestures and actions looked quite unlike those of a thief.

Listener's Response

Name _____

Fable 2: One person reads aloud while others listen.

Short Sightedness
A joke of the nineteenth century by an unknown author

Two men were short-sighted, but instead of admitting it, both of them boasted of keen vision. One day they heard that a tablet was to be hung in a temple. So each of them found out what was written on it beforehand. When the day came, they both went to the temple. Looking up, one said, "Look, aren't the characters 'Brightness and Uprighteousness'?" "And the smaller ones. There! You can't see them, they say, 'Written by so and so in a certain month, on a certain day'!" said the other. A passer-by asked what they were looking at. When told, the man laughed. "The tablet hasn't been hoisted up, so how can you see the characters?" he asked.

Listener's Response

Fable 3: One person reads while others listen.

The Lord Who Loved Dragons
Shen Zi (The works of Shen Buhai of the fourth century B.C.)

Lord She was so fond of dragons that he had them painted and carved all over his house. When the real dragon in heaven heard about this, it flew down and put its head through Lord She's door and its tail through one of his windows. When the lord saw this, he fled, frightened nearly out of his wits. This shows that the lord was not really fond of dragons. He liked all that looked like dragons, but not the genuine thing.

Listener's Response

Name _____

Enriching Understanding through Small-Group Negotiation

How often have you been asked to read or listen to something and offer your response, only to discover that you had very little to say because you did not really understand what you had read or heard? Group discussion can help you to get more out of what you hear because the group as a whole can remember more details and generate many more insights than any single person can. The following activity will demonstrate with a poem how valuable group sharing can be.

1. Create groups of six people.
2. One person in the group reads the following poem aloud while others listen.

Style

by Carl Sandburg

Style—go ahead talking about style.
You can tell where a man gets his style just
    as you can tell where Pavlova* got her legs
    or Ty Cobb his batting eye.

  Go on talking.
Only don't take my style away.
    It's my face.
    Maybe no good
        but anyway, my face.
I talk with it, I sing with it, I see, taste and feel with it,
    I know why I want to keep it.

Kill my style
    and you break Pavlova's legs,
    and you blind Ty Cobb's batting eye.

*[Pavlova was a famous Russian ballerina]

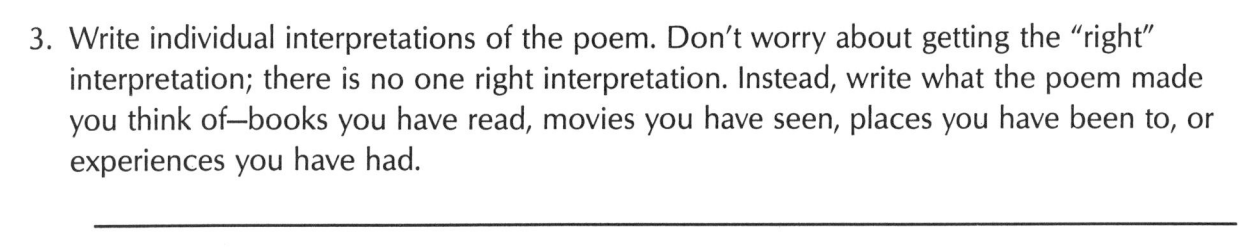

3. Write individual interpretations of the poem. Don't worry about getting the "right" interpretation; there is no one right interpretation. Instead, write what the poem made you think of—books you have read, movies you have seen, places you have been to, or experiences you have had.

_____
_____
_____

Name _____

4. Within the group of six, create three sets of partners. Read your response notes to your partner, and have your partner read his or her notes to you. On the following lines, write down anything in your partner's response that helped you to see more possibilities in the poem.

_____
_____
_____

5. Join with the other students in your group of six. Have each person read his or her response to the poem. Once again, list any additional ideas from these responses that helped you to see more possibilities in the poem.

_____
_____
_____

6. Share everyone's interpretations with the entire class.

7. Finally, write your revised interpretation of Sandburg's poem, "Style."

_____
_____
_____
_____
_____

8. Share your revised interpretations. Discuss with the class how group sharing affected your understanding of the poem.

Speech and Lecture Notes

Name _____

Sometimes listening may seem like a passive activity in which a listener simply relaxes and absorbs what a speaker is saying. Nothing could be further from the truth. In some ways listeners have to work harder than readers or even speakers. Good listeners have to do two things almost at the same time: (1) they have to listen to what the speaker says, and (2) they must draw on their experience and knowledge to make sense of what the speaker has said. Furthermore, they must make these connections very quickly. Everyone has had the experience of listening to a speaker and suddenly realizing that they have no idea what the person has said. It is not that the mind has been inactive; rather, it has probably been very active on thoughts triggered by something the speaker has said. Imagine that you are listening to someone talking about dogs. What possible associations having to do with dogs might you make if your mind began to wander—dogs you have known, movies or books about dogs, etc.? List several associations on the lines below.

_____   _____

_____   _____

_____   _____

If you had been reading a story, you would have been free to think as long and as much as you want about this dog, because when you were ready, you could go back to the story to find out about the dog in the story. However, if you were listening to someone talking about a dog, you would need to cut your recollections short and return immediately to what the speaker was saying. Otherwise you would be in danger of missing important and irretrievable information. When you find your mind wandering too far and too long, you can increase your concentration by doing one or more of the following:

- predict what the speaker will say next
- make outline notes
- develop questions
- summarize what has been said

Try It!

Watch an informative video from an educational television program, public broadcasting station, or news channel.

- Try the four strategies above for improving concentration.
- Take notes on some of the thoughts and associations that interrupt your concentration.
- Discuss your experience with the class.

Name _____

Using Prediction and Outlining to Enhance Listening

One strategy you can use to keep your attention focused on a speaker's message is to outline the speaker's main points and predict what will be said next. Prepare three-minute informative speeches for the following activity. Include a title, introduction, body with several main points, and conclusion. Stop briefly after each part to allow listeners to fill in their responses in the lines below.

1. **Speaker:** read the title.
   Audience: predict what the speech will be about.
   _____

2. **Speaker:** read the introduction.
   Audience: predict what the main point or purpose of the speech will be.
   _____
   _____

3. **Speaker:** read the body of the speech.
   Audience: outline key ideas.

   Key Idea _____

   Key Idea _____

   Key Idea _____

   Key Idea _____

4. **Speaker:** read the conclusion.
   Audience: predict what the speaker will say in the conclusion.
   _____

5. Compare outlines with class members.

Name _____

Listening to Interpret

An important part of listening is not just to recall what the speaker said, but to determine what the speaker meant. Once again, take turns giving three-minute, informative speeches. Speakers should prepare written "Speaker's Notes"—outlines of key points that they want to make (use the guide below). As speakers present their speeches, listeners identify what they hear, using the "Listener's Notes" below as a guide. After each speech has been presented, listeners will compare their notes with those of the speaker.

Speaker's Notes/Listener's Notes

Speaker _____ Listener _____

Speech Title _____

Introduction/Purpose of the Speech (what the speaker wants the audience to learn, believe)
_____
_____
_____

Key Idea _____

Key Idea _____

Key Idea _____

Key Idea _____

Conclusion (what speaker wants audience to think or do) _____
_____
_____
_____

Name _____

Listening to Evaluate

In addition to recalling what a speaker has said and making some determination about what the speaker meant, active listeners also evaluate the worth of what the speaker said and the skill with which the speaker said it. They ask themselves, "Is this accurate? Appropriate? Convincing? Was this pleasing in its presentation?" Take turns giving three-minute, informative speeches. Listeners evaluate the presentations using the "Listener's Response Sheet" below.

Listener's Response Sheet

Speaker _____ Listener _____

Speech Title _____

Introduction/Purpose of the Speech (what the speaker wants the audience to learn, believe)
_____
_____
_____

What were the most convincing points?
_____
_____
_____

What was the least convincing? Why?
_____
_____
_____

General Observations—Appropriateness for Audience, Purpose, and Occasion
Place a ✓+ (excellent), ✓ (satisfactory), or ✓- (needs improvement) on the line following each.

choice of topic _____   use of language _____   body language _____

supporting detail _____   personal appearance _____   vocal expression _____

Comments about overall presentation _____
_____

Stories and Poems

Listening for Pleasure

Although much of the listening that you do is intended to provide information, other listening is purely for pleasure. For example, interesting stories enable you to go on imaginary adventures. Poems let you find your deepest thoughts expressed eloquently. These pleasurable listening experiences enable you to learn more about yourself and in various ways enrich your life. When you listen actively, you find that you are constantly making personal associations, predicting what will come next, and confirming, rejecting, or revising those predictions as the story unfolds. The following activity will demonstrate these listeners' responses and provide some strategies for making your listening even more enjoyable. As the teacher reads the story, you will be asked at various points to comment on your responses.

Section 1: Teacher Reads

To Build a Fire (1902 version)
by Jack London

For land travel or seafaring, the world over, a companion is usually considered desirable. In the Klondike, as Tom Vincent found out, such a companion is absolutely essential. But he found it out, not by precept, but through bitter experience.

"Never travel alone," is a precept of the north. He had heard it many times and laughed: for he was a strapping young fellow, big-boned and big-muscled, with faith in himself and in the strength of his head and hands.

It was on a bleak January day when the experience came that taught him respect for the frost and for the wisdom of the men who had battled with it.

He had left Calumet Camp on the Yukon with a light pack on his back, to go up Paul Creek to the divide between it and Cherry Creek, where his party was prospecting and hunting moose.

The frost was sixty degrees below zero, and he had thirty miles of lonely trail to cover, but he did not mind. In fact, he enjoyed it, swinging along through the silence, his blood pounding warmly through his veins, and his mind carefree and happy. For he and his comrades were certain they had struck "pay" up there on the Cherry Creek Divide; and, further, he was returning to them from Dawson with cheery home letters from the States.

Listener's Response
1. What is the situation at the beginning of this story?
2. What character(s) have been introduced?
3. Where is the story taking place?
4. Can you roughly establish the historical time in which the story takes place? What details help you?
5. What details particularly catch your attention?
6. If you were going on an adventure, where would it be? Would you go alone or take someone with you? Who?
7. What do you expect will happen in this story? Why?

Section 2: Teacher Reads

At seven o'clock, when he turned the heels of his moccasins toward Calumet Camp, it was still black night. And when day broke at half past nine he had made the four-mile cut-off across the flats and was six miles up Paul Creek. The trail, which had seen little travel, followed the bed of the creek, and there was no possibility of his getting lost. He had gone to Dawson by way of Cherry Creek and Indian River, so Paul Creek was new and strange. By half past eleven he was at the forks, which had been described to him, and he knew he had covered fifteen miles, half the distance.

He knew that in the nature of things the trail was bound to grow worse from there on, and thought that, considering the good time he had made, he merited lunch. Casting off his pack and taking a seat on a fallen tree, he unmittened his right hand, reached inside his shirt next to the skin, and fished out a couple of biscuits sandwiched with sliced bacon and wrapped in a handkerchief—the only way they could be carried without freezing solid.

He had barely chewed the first mouthful when his numbing fingers warned him to put his mitten on again. This he did, not without surprise at the bitter swiftness with which the frost bit in. Undoubtedly it was the coldest snap he had ever experienced, he thought.

He spat upon the snow,—a favorite northland trick,—and the sharp crackle of the instantly congealed spittle startled him. The spirit thermometer at Calumet had registered sixty below when he left, but he was certain it had grown much colder, how much colder he could not imagine.

Half of the first biscuit was yet untouched, but he could feel himself beginning to chill—a thing most unusual for him. This would never do he decided, and slipping the pack-straps across his shoulders, he leaped to his feet and ran briskly up the trail.

A few minutes of this made him warm again, and he settled down to a steady stride, munching the biscuits as he went along. The moisture that exhaled with his breath crusted his lips and mustache with pendent ice and formed a miniature glacier on his chin. Now and again sensation forsook his nose and cheeks, and he rubbed them till they burned with the returning blood.

Most men wore nose-straps; his partners did, but he had scorned such "feminine contraptions," and till now had never felt the need of them. Now he did feel the need, for he was rubbing constantly.

Nevertheless he was aware of a thrill of joy, of exultation. He was doing something, achieving something, mastering the elements. Once he laughed aloud in sheer strength of life, and with his clenched fist defied the frost. He was its master. What he did, he did in spite of it. It could not stop him. He was going on to the Cherry Creek Divide.

Strong as were the elements, he was stronger. At such times animals crawled away into their holes and remained in hiding. But he did not hide. He was out in it, facing it, fighting it. He was a man, a master of things.

In such fashion, rejoicing proudly, he tramped on. After half an hour he rounded a bend, where the creek ran close to the mountainside, and came upon one of the most insignificant-appearing but most formidable dangers in northern travel.

The creek itself was frozen solid to its rocky bottom, but from the mountain came the outflow of several springs. These springs never froze, and the only effect of the severest cold snaps was to lessen their discharge. Protected from the frost by the blanket of snow, the water of these springs seeped down into the creek, and, on top of the creek ice, formed shallow pools.

The surface of these pools, in turn, took on a skin of ice which grew thicker and thicker, until the water overran, and so formed a second ice-skinned pool above the first.

Thus at the bottom was the solid creek ice, then probably six to eight inches of water, then a thin ice-skin, then another six inches of water and another ice-skin. And on top of this last skin was about an inch of recent snow to make the trap complete.

Listener's Response

1. Have you changed your expectation? Explain your answer.
2. What kind of person is Tom Vincent? Find passages to support your view.
3. What experiences in your own life does this story remind you of? Have you ever taken risks against the advice of other people? What happened?
4. What do you think will happen next?

Section 3: Teacher Reads

To Tom Vincent's eye the unbroken snow surface gave no warning of the lurking danger. As the crust was thicker at the edge, he was well toward the middle before he broke through.

In itself it was a very insignificant mishap,—a man does not drown in twelve inches of water,—but in its consequences as serious an accident as could possibly befall him.

At the instant he broke through he felt the cold water strike his feet and ankles, and with half a dozen lunges he made the bank. He was quite cool and collected. The thing to do, and the only thing to do, was to build a fire. For another precept of the north runs: *Travel with wet socks down to twenty below zero; after that build a fire.* And it was three times twenty below and colder, and he knew it.

He knew, further, that great care must be exercised; that with failure at the first attempt, the chance was made greater for failure at the second attempt. In short, he knew that there must be no failure. The moment before a strong, exulting man, boastful of his mastery of the elements, he was now fighting for his life against those same elements—such was the difference caused by the injection of a quart of water into a northland traveller's calculations.

In a clump of pines on the rim of the bank the spring high-water had lodged many twigs and small branches. Thoroughly dried by the summer sun, they now waited the match.

It is impossible to build a fire with heavy Alaskan mittens on one's hands, so Vincent bared his, gathered a sufficient number of twigs, and knocking the snow from them, knelt down to kindle his fire. From an inside pocket he drew out his matches and a strip of thin birch bark. The matches were of the Klondike kind, sulphur matches, one hundred in a bunch.

He noticed how quickly his fingers had chilled as he separated one match from the bunch and scratched it on his trousers. The birch bark, like the driest of paper, burst into bright flame. This he carefully fed with the smallest twigs and finest debris, cherishing the flame with the utmost care. It did not do to hurry things, as he well knew, and although his fingers were now quite stiff, he did not hurry.

After the first quick, biting sensation of cold, his feet had ached with a heavy, dull ache and were rapidly growing numb. But the fire, although a very young one, was now a success, and he knew that a little snow, briskly rubbed, would speedily cure his feet.

Listener's Response

1. Describe or draw what you visualize in your mind at this point.
2. What do you expect will happen now? Explain your answer.

Section 4: Teacher Reads

But at the moment he was adding the first thick twigs to the fire, a grievous thing happened. The pine boughs above his head were burdened with a four months' snowfall, and so finely adjusted were the burdens that his light movements in collecting the twigs had been sufficient to disturb the balance.

The snow from the topmost bough was the first to fall, striking and dislodging the snow on the boughs beneath. And all this snow, accumulating as it fell, smote Tom Vincent's head and shoulders and blotted out his fire.

He still kept his presence of mind, for he knew how great his danger was. He started at once to rebuild the fire, but his fingers were now so cold that he could not bend them, and he was forced to pick up each twig and splinter between the tips of the fingers of either hand.

When he came to the match he encountered great difficulty in separating one from the bunch. This he succeeded in managing, however, and also, by a great effort, in clutching the match between his thumb and forefinger. But in scratching it, he dropped it in the snow and could not pick it up again.

He stood up, desperate. He could not feel even his weight on his feet, although the ankles were aching painfully. Putting on his mittens, he stepped to one side, so that the snow would not fall upon the new fire he was to build, and beat his hands violently against a tree-trunk.

This enabled him to separate and strike a second match and to set fire to the remaining fragment of birch bark. But his body had now begun to chill and he was shivering, so that when he tried to add the first twigs his hand shook and the tiny flame was quenched.

The frost had beaten him. His hands were worthless. But he had the foresight to drop the bunch of matches into his wide-mouthed outside pocket before he slipped on his mittens in despair and started to run up the trail. One cannot run the frost out of wet feet at sixty below and colder, however, as he quickly discovered.

He came round a sharp turn of the creek to where he could look ahead for a mile. But there was no help, no sign of help, only the white trees and the white hills, the quiet cold and the brazen silence! If only he had a comrade whose feet were not freezing, he thought, only such a comrade to start the fire that could save him!

Then his eyes chanced upon another high-water lodgment of twigs and leaves and branches. If he could strike a match, all might yet be well. With stiff fingers which he could not bend, he got out a bunch of matches, but found it impossible to separate them.

He sat down and awkwardly shuffled the bunch about on his knees, until he got it resting on his palm with the sulphur ends projecting, somewhat in the manner of the blade of a hunting-knife would project when clutched in the fist.

But his fingers stood straight out. They could not clutch. This he overcame by pressing the wrist of the other hand against them, and so forcing them down upon the bunch. Time and again, holding thus by both hands, he scratched the bunch on his leg and finally ignited it. But the flame burned into the flesh of his hand, and he involuntarily relaxed his hold. The bunch fell into the snow, and while he tried vainly to pick it up, sizzled and went out.

Listener's Response

1. Have you changed your expectation? If so, how and why? If not, what has happened to confirm your earlier prediction?
2. What would you do next if you were Tom Vincent?

Section 5: Teacher Reads

Again he ran, by this time badly frightened. His feet were utterly devoid of sensation. He stubbed his toes once on a buried log, but beyond pitching him into the snow and wrenching his back, it gave him no feelings.

His fingers were helpless and his wrists were beginning to grow numb. His nose and cheeks he knew were freezing but they did not count. It was his feet and hands that were to save him, if he was to be saved.

He recollected being told of a camp of moose-hunters somewhere above the forks of Paul Creek. He must be somewhere near it, he thought, and if he could find it he yet might be saved. Five minutes later he came upon it, lone and deserted, with drifted snow sprinkled inside the pine-bough shelter in which the hunters had slept. He sank down, sobbing. All was over. In an hour at best, in that terrific temperature, he would be an icy corpse.

But the love of life was strong in him and he sprang again to his feet. He was thinking quickly. What if the matches did burn his hands? Burned hands were better than dead hands. No hands at all were better than death. He floundered along the trail till he came upon another high-water lodgement. There were twigs and branches, leaves and grasses dry and waiting the fire.

Again he sat down and shuffled the bunch of matches on his knees, got it into place on his palm, with the wrist of his other hand forced nerveless fingers down against the bunch, and with the wrist kept them there. At the second scratch the bunch caught fire, and he knew that if he could stand the pain he was saved. He choked with the sulphur fumes, and the blue flame licked the flesh of his hands.

Listener's Response

1. What do you expect will happen? Explain your answer.

Name _____

Section 6: Teacher Reads

At first he could not feel it, but it burned quickly in through the frosted surface. The odor of the burning flesh—his flesh—was strong in his nostrils. He writhed about in his torment, yet held on. He set his teeth and swayed back and forth, until the clear white flame of the burning match shot up, and he had applied that flame to the leaves and grasses.

An anxious five minutes followed, but the fire gained steadily. Then he set to work to save himself. Heroic measures were necessary, such was his extremity, and he took them.

Alternately rubbing his hands with snow and thrusting them into the flames, and now and again beating them against the hard trees, he restored their circulation sufficiently for them to be of use to him. With his hunting-knife he slashed the straps from his pack, unrolled his blanket, and got out dry socks and foot-gear.

Then he cut away his moccasins and bared his feet. But while he had taken liberties with his hands, he kept his feet fairly away from the fire and rubbed them with snow. He rubbed till his hand grew numb, when he would cover his feet with the blanket, warm his hands by the fire, and return to the rubbing.

For three hours he worked, till the worst effects of the freezing had been counteracted. All that night he stayed by the fire, and it was late the next day when he limped pitifully into the camp on the Cherry Creek Divide.

In a month's time he was able to be about on his feet, although the toes were destined always after that to be very sensitive to frost. But the scars on his hands he knows he will carry *to* the grave. And —"*Never travel alone!*" he now lays down the precept of the north.

Listener's Response

1. Are you surprised that Tom Vincent survived?

2. Based on what you know about Tom Vincent, how do you think he will change as a result of this experience? Explain your answer.

3. Write a theme statement for the story. (Theme statements usually make statements about what life is like rather than what people should do.)

   _____

   _____

4. Reread your responses to each section of this story. Compare your responses with those of classmates. Did you have similar or different expectations at each point in the story? What experiences in your lives may have contributed to different expectations? List on the board all of the various theme statements that you and your classmates find in the story.

5. Write a story telling of an experience that frightened you. Following Jack London's pattern in "To Build a Fire," include the following in your story:
   - tell who the characters were
   - tell where and when the incident happened
   - tell the details of what happened
   - tell how the incident was resolved

6. Read your story to classmates. At one key point in the story, stop reading and ask classmates to predict the ending.

Listening to Poetry

Finding meaning in poetry is sometimes easier if you do not try too hard to interpret it on the first reading. Instead, if you allow yourself to create mental pictures and look for words that seem to have special meaning, you will find yourself gradually becoming more successful at discovering meaning and enjoying poetry even more. Your teacher will read aloud the following poem, one stanza at a time. After each stanza answer these questions:

1. What image do you see? Describe or draw it.
2. What word or words stand out to you? Support your choice. (Because every word is important, there are no wrong choices.)
3. What is happening in this stanza? Describe it briefly.

After the entire poem has been read aloud, share images, list selected words on the board, and share descriptions for each stanza. Then, individually or as a class, write sentences suggesting points that the poet may be making in the poem.

Blight
by Edna St. Vincent Millay

1

Hard seeds of hate I planted
    That should by now be grown,
Rough stalks, and from thick stamens
    A poisonous pollen blown,
And odors rank, unbreathable,
    From dark corollas thrown!

2

At dawn from my damp garden
    I shook the chilly dew;
The thin boughs locked behind me
    That sprang to let me through;
The blossom slept,—I sought a place
    Where nothing lovely grew.

3

And there, when day was breaking,
    I knelt and looked around:
The light was near, the silence
    Was palpitant with sound;
I drew my hate from out my breast
    And thrust it in the ground.

4

O, ye so fiercely tended,
    Ye little seeds of hate!
I bent above your growing
    Early and noon and late,
Yet are ye drooped and pitiful,—
    I cannot rear ye straight!

5

The sun seeks out my garden,
    No nook is left in shade,
No mist nor mold nor mildew
    Endures on any blade,
Sweet rain slants under every bough:
    Ye falter, and ye fade.

Name _____

Broadcast Media

Advertising

Much of what you hear and see on radio and television is intended to sell you something—whether it is a product, a service, or an idea. Often these messages are very subtle, so that you may not immediately recognize that you are being persuaded to do or think something. Your job as a listener is to critically analyze the message and its value to you. One way that you can be a savvy consumer is to ask yourself questions about what is claimed and who might benefit from your action. Below are two advertising situations.

- **A movie star wearing a doctor's jacket telling listeners that a particular pain medication is superior to other brands.**
- **An athlete recommending a particular beverage or food for creating stamina.**

Apply the following listening questions to each situation.
1. What is the speaker's primary purpose (to entertain, inform, or persuade)?
2. Is the speaker qualified to speak on this topic? Why or why not?
3. Who, if anyone, benefits from having you respond a certain way?
4. What are the alternatives? Would they be as good?

Advertisers use various types of appeals. Following are some common ones. See whether you can find at least three of the following appeals on radio or television. Circle the type of appeal, identify the service or product, and briefly describe the advertisement.

Type of Appeal	Service or Product	Description
sex appeal	_____	_____
plain folks	_____	_____
appeal to tradition	_____	_____
appeal to authority	_____	_____
snob appeal	_____	_____
something for nothing	_____	_____
everyone else has one	_____	_____
another _____	_____	_____

© Instructional Fair • TS Denison   91   IF19304 Writing, Speaking, and Listening

Name _____

Television Shows and Movies

In some ways movies and television shows are a lot like advertising. Instead of selling products, though, they sell ideas—ideas about what life is like or what people value. As with advertising, we need to be aware of these messages and critically analyze their accuracy and worth. In the spaces below list three of your favorite television shows and three of your favorite movies. Then check the blanks in each category that best describe your choices.

	TV Show	TV Show	TV Show	Movie	Movie	Movie
What is the type?						
Comedy						
Drama						
Action or thriller						
Science fiction						
Romance						
Educational						
Who is the hero?						
Male						
Female						
Minority						
What is the hero like?						
Complex (shows both strength and weakness)						
Stereotyped (one-sided, usually no weakness)						
What is valued?						
Physical beauty						
Wealth						
Violence						
Intelligence						
Kindness						
Hard work						
Honesty						
What is the effect?						
Teaches insight about life						
No insight—not realistic						

1. What similarities do you see in your favorite shows and movies? Summarize your choices.
2. How does life in these films or movies differ from the world you live in?
3. How realistically and fairly are specific groups portrayed (for example, minorities, men, women, children, poor people)?